2nd ARMORED DIVISION
'Hell on Wheels'

An M10 Tank Destroyer along with troops of the 30th
Infantry Division prepare for the final assault on
Magdeburg on April 17, 1945.
U.S. Army via Real War Photos

SPEARHEAD

2nd ARMORED DIVISION
'Hell on Wheels'

Steven Smith

Ian Allan
PUBLISHING

Right: 2nd Armored Division's war: from Northwest Africa to Berlin. *The maps and all other artwork were produced by Mark Franklin of Flatt Artt*

Acknowledgements

The author would like to express gratitude a number of individuals who made this work possible. First thanks go to Simon Forty for his organisational brilliance. Samuel Southworth likewise provided excellent assistance and expertise, as did Mark Bando, whose knowledge of the 2nd Armored matches his well known expertise on the 101st Airborne. Dr. Robert Cameron, Armored Historian at Ft. Knox, generously provided advice, as did historian Richard Killblane and Tim Renick, head of the U.S. Army Transportation School Info Center. Donald Sommerville has lent his excellent editing skill to the manuscript. Sincerest thanks go to CMH-winner James Burt, Roscoe ('Rockie') Blunt, Brett Vinson, Kal Isaacs and James Provens, via his son Timothy, who has carefully preserved his dad's experiences in WWII for the benefit of future generations. On the illustrative side, thanks to Mark Bando, Chris Ellis, Mark Franklin, George Forty and Tim Hawkins.

First published 2003

ISBN 0 7110 2976 8

Published by Ian Allan Ltd

an imprint of Ian Allan Publishing Ltd, Hersham, Surrey KT12 4RG
Printed by Ian Allan Printing Ltd, Hersham, Surrey KT12 4RG

Code: 0306/B

British Library Cataloguing in Publication Data
A CIP catalogue record for this book is available from the British Library

Note: Internet site information provided in the Reference section was correct when provided by the author. The publisher can accept no responsibility for this information becoming incorrect.

Abbreviations

2AD	2nd Armored Division	CO	Commanding officer	Mot Inf	Motorised infantry
AAA	Anti-aircraft artillery	Co (s)	Company (companies)	MP	Military Police
AB	Airborne	Col	Column	OD	Olive drab
AEF	American Expeditionary Force	CP	Command post	QM	Quartermaster
		Coy	Company	Pfc/Pvt	Private (first class)
AF in G	American Forces in Germany	Det	Detachment	Pl	Platoon
		ea	each	RCT	Regimental Combat Team
Amb	Ambulance	Engr	Engineer	Recce/Recon	Reconnaissance
Armd	Armored	ETO	European Theater of Operations	Regt	Regiment
Arty	Artillery			RHQ	Regimental HQ
asst	Assistant	Fd Arty	Field artillery	Sect	Section
A/tk	Anti-tank	HBT	Herringbone twill	(T or S/) Sgt	(Technical or Staff/) Sergeant
Bn	Battalion	HMG	Heavy MG (.50 cal)	SHAEF	Supreme HQ Allied Powers in Europe
BR	British	Hy	Heavy		
Brig	Brigade	Inf	Infantry	Sig	Signals
Bty	Battery	LMG	Light MG (.30 cal)	SP	Self-propelled
camo	camouflage	LST	Landing Ship Tank	Tac	Tactical
cal	caliber	Lt	Light	Tk	Tank
Cav	Cavalry	(1-/2-) Lt	(First/Second) Lieutenant	USAAF	U.S. Army Air Force
CC (A/B)	Combat Command (A/B)	Maint	Maintenance	USMC	U.S. Marine Corps
C-in-C	Commander-in-Chief	MC	Motorcycle	Veh	Vehicle
CG	Commanding general	(G/H)MC	(Gun/howitzer) motor carriage		
Cml	Chemical	Med	Medium or Medical		
		MG	Machine gun		

CONTENTS

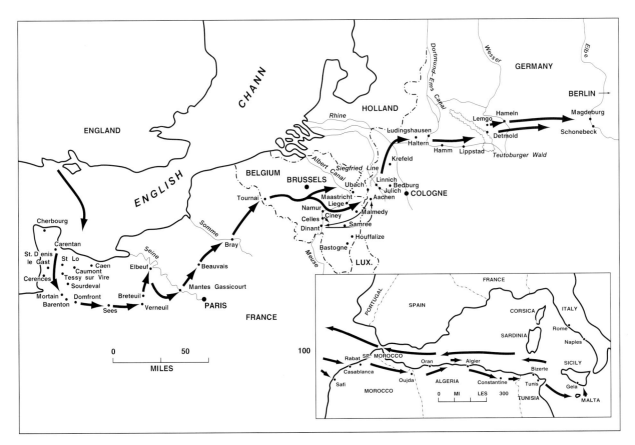

ORIGINS & HISTORY

The 2nd Armored Division was the direct descendant of the U.S. Tank Corps of World War I. This was America's first armored unit, formed to stand alongside British and French armored forces, which had shown that the tank might possibly be the answer to the murderous infantry and artillery deadlock on the Western Front.

After a disappearance of about 400 years, the massed armored charge had reappeared in Europe at the Battle of Cambrai in November 1917. The attack, from out of a dawn mist, of nearly 350 Allied tanks surprised the Germans, and their formerly impenetrable front caved in for three miles. For a short time it appeared as if the Western Allies had invented a war-winning weapon. But, stripped of surprise, the early tanks could not best heavy firepower, and ten days later the Germans counterattacked, reclaiming the lost ground along with about 180 destroyed or abandoned machines.

Nevertheless the tank pointed to the future of warfare, and the Americans, using French vehicles, were quick to form their own armored units. A cavalryman who had grown restless on General John Pershing's staff, Major George Patton, became the driving force behind America's tank effort. He not only organized and trained the new Tank Corps but fought on the front line, receiving a wound during the Meuse-Argonne battle and awards for gallantry. His wound had actually been received when he was on foot, looking for help for some of his machines that had become mired in mud.

During the war, as many problems as solutions had emerged from the use of tanks. For one thing they were slow — with a top speed of 4mph hardly able to keep up with a trotting rifleman — and they were unable to penetrate obstacles, such as holes in the ground, woods or streams, that were easily passed by infantry. Initial models were also huge, up to nine men rattling along inside the ponderous contraptions, so they were very simple targets for German artillery. (Others were so small as to be completely unformidable.) The biggest problem for the Great War tanks was that firepower technology was already at an advanced stage, due to naval battles where all sides had already studied how to penetrate armor. In order to be mobile at all, initial tanks needed to have very thin armor, which, along with the tanks' propensity for mechanical breakdowns, presented a field day to any enemy weapons that could get a clear shot. For a brief period, the heavy machine gun served as an excellent anti-tank weapon.

The British had first introduced tanks in desperation in September 1916 during their disastrous offensive on the Somme, where the machines frightened no one but their occupants. Cambrai provided a hint of their usefulness, and then the Battle of Amiens in August 1918 seemed to reveal them as a trump. Again, hundreds of tanks churned forward at dawn and this time the entire German line collapsed, calling it quits. Following their armor, thousands of Allied troops made unprecedented gains. It was called the "Black Day" of the German Army. Of course since Germany was by then on the brink of material, physical and moral collapse, it was suggested afterward that a crowd of maids waving feather dusters could have collapsed the enemy front just as rapidly. It was not

Below: A 2nd Armored dispatch rider mounted on a Harley-Davidson WLA motorcycle. This was one of two militarized variants of the prewar 750cc side-valve engined WL—the WLA (for Army) was supplied to both American and Chinese armies; the WLC differed only in details and was originally built for Canada but went on to see use by Russia, Britain, and Commonwealth forces. Harley built more than 88,000 machines during the war and earned a special award from the U.S. Army for doing so. WLA and WLCs went on to become the standard mount of military policemen, other military motorcycle riders, and despatch riders. *Courtesy of Mark Bando*

clear at all whether tanks had achieved the breakthrough or whether the Germans — for numerous other reasons — had simply thrown in the towel.

After the Great War, the American doughboys returned home, less 117,000 dead, to find their country swept by isolationist sentiment. In 1920 the United States Tank Corps was disbanded and Patton, among others, returned to the horse cavalry. The original tank battalions were shuffled through a series of organizational shifts and nomenclature until on October 25, 1932, in their latest incarnation, the 1st Tank Regiment, they were converted and redesignated the 66th Infantry Regiment (Light Tanks). A sister formation invented in 1929, the 2nd Tank Regiment, was renamed the 67th Infantry Regiment (Medium Tanks).

It was not that tanks had failed to prove their usefulness in the Great War — in fact, used in mass they had seemed an excellent bludgeon against enemy defense lines. It was more that none of the Allies foresaw being placed once again on the strategic offensive. France devoted most of its energy to constructing a system of static fortifications, the Maginot Line, along its border with Germany. Britain saw its best promise in the concept of strategic bombing, meant, like the French fortifications, to be a deterrent.

In the United States, where fears of land invasion were nonexistent, armor became a military backwater, pulled between the infantry and cavalry, neither of whom really wanted it. The cavalry clung stubbornly to its horses (and swords, boots and riding pants) while the infantry was convinced that the only possible use for tanks was to assist the efforts of the foot soldier. An independent armored force that could undertake separate operations was considered foolish, if not heretical.

Nevertheless, motor technology, in the air as well as on the ground, progressed rapidly during the 1930s, and both the cavalry and infantry were forced to admit vehicles with new potential into their services. A series of maneuvers in Kansas pitting horses against armored cars, ended decisively in favor of the machines. The cavalry reluctantly began to mechanize some of its units. When the fully tracked M2A2 began to appear in 1934, it was called the "Combat Car," so as not to be confuse it with an "infantry" tank. Elsewhere, sentiment held that tanks should support the infantry, not the other way around.

The argument polarized around two beliefs: one was that tanks, if they had to happen at all, were to be the modern successors of cavalry — fast and nimble, able to perform reconnaissance, raids, or exploitation of a retreating enemy. The other belief, forged through the front-line massacres of the Great War, held that tanks should be heavily armored, lumbering big brothers to the infantry, accompanying them at their own pace into battle, or perhaps standing as resolute rocks in defense.

Not only the Americans but the British and French (and Russians, who, as the Soviets, immediately began building as many tanks as they could) subscribed to the same general view. Cavalry would gradually be mechanized, though it would retain the same functions as always; while the infantry would be buttressed — not replaced — by tanks that could accompany them into battle.

The victors of World War I thus clung to their war-winning systems, only reluctantly incorporating new armor developments into their schemes. The only great power that readily embraced the concept of tanks was the loser in the Great War, Germany.

When Hitler took power in 1933 he began a crash program to rebuild Germany's

Above: Medium M2 of the 2nd Armored Division during the 1941 Louisiana Maneuvers. Note the exercise identification cross. The M2 was most noteworthy as the vehicle from which the M3 medium was developed. As the M2's 37mm main gun was rendered obsolete by German Panzer IIIs and IVs in 1940, it was essential for U.S. armor to keep pace. A hasty redesign of the M2A1 proposal led to the M3 medium, with its sponson-mounted 75mm gun. This, in turn, led to Chrysler's order for 1,000 M2A1s being cancelled and replaced by one for the M3. In the end under 100 M2A1s were built in 1940–41 and used only for training in the U.S. *Via Chris Ellis*

might from scratch. Since an entrenched military bureaucracy no longer existed, his Nazi regime was free to adopt new ideas — particularly those of Germany's leading tank expert, Heinz Guderian — and arm its new legions with the most modern available equipment. The Germans gambled on an independent armored force, grouping tanks into self-standing divisions with their own specialized armored infantry and reconnaissance units. Aside from motorized or self-propelled artillery, the tanks would receive fire support from Germany's other innovation, the dive bomber. The Germans' new concept of warfare would be called "Blitzkrieg," or lightning war.

On September 1, 1939, the Germans began World War II in Europe by invading Poland. Their five Panzer divisions sliced through the front, devastating rear areas while executing huge encirclements of front-line Polish forces. Instead of an interminable slugging match along Great War lines, the campaign was decided in three weeks. Afterward, the Germans dismissed their own tentative experiment with "light" armored divisions, converting these to full Panzer divisions, relying on captured Czech tanks.

It cannot be said that Germany's demolition of the fledgling state of Poland caused any panic in Western military councils. The French and British had manufactured more tanks than the Wehrmacht, and the combined Allied strength was not to be confused with that of Poland should the Germans turn west. Nevertheless, this first example of Blitzkrieg caused some tremors, and in January 1940 the French began organizing their disparate battalions of infantry and cavalry tanks into three armored divisions. The British also started assembling their first.

On May 10, 1940, the Germans invaded west with 10 Panzer divisions, eight of them grouped together and aimed at vulnerable points in French defenses along the Meuse River. In less than a month the British Army was forced to flee from the Continent, leaving all of its equipment behind. France, holding a southern stub of its territory, requested an armistice with the Germans, which took effect on June 25, 1940. According to Omar Bradley, "Militarily, the Nazi forces had operated with awesome efficiency. The coordination between air and ground, tanks and motorized infantry, exceeded anything we had ever dreamed of in the U.S. Army."

Three weeks later, on July 15, 1940, the United States activated its 1st and 2nd Armored Divisions. All debate came to a halt. The U.S. needed its own armored force.

In a reflection of the former tug-of-war between the cavalry and infantry branches, the 1st Armored Division was built around the 7th Cavalry Brigade (Mechanized) and the 2nd Armored was built around a provisional brigade consisting of the 66th Infantry Regiment (Light Tanks) and 67th Infantry Regiment (Medium Tanks). Conversely, the 1st Armored's initial commander was an infantryman, General Bruce Magruder, while the 2nd was commanded by a cavalryman, General Charles L. Scott. The 2nd Armored was assigned to Ft. Benning, Georgia, which housed the Infantry School and the 4th Infantry Division, and the 1st Armored was based at Ft. Knox, Kentucky, which housed the new Armor School. It would turn out that the 1st Armored was disadvantaged by being based at Ft. Knox, where cadre was spread in all directions. The 2nd Armored at Ft. Benning was able to train with less distraction.

In terms of lineage, while the 1st Armored inherited the finest traditions of the U.S. cavalry, including the 1st Cavalry Regiment, the 2nd Armored, through the 66th Infantry, became the direct offspring of the U.S. Tank Corps in World War I. Less than two weeks after its founding it inherited another legacy of that corps, when Colonel George S. Patton arrived to command the 2nd Armored's tank brigade.

At the time of its activation, the 2nd Armored had only 99 officers and 2,202 men, from an authorized complement of nearly 10,000. Due to its home in Georgia — or to the famous Confederate preference for riding instead of walking — the division's first recruits came primarily from the South. By 1941, once the national draft had kicked in,

Above: M2A4s of Companies F and C, 66th Armored Regiment, during the Tennessee Maneuvers in June 1941. *Via Chris Ellis*

the division filled out with men from throughout the United States. At first the 2nd Armored was ill-supplied with equipment as well as men and Scott, as profane an old coot as Patton, had to lobby hard for weapons, spare parts, and even uniforms.

On November 3, 1940, General Scott was promoted to command the U.S. I Armor Corps (1st and 2nd Armored), and George Patton took over the 2AD. With his usual touch of flair, Patton quickly organized a 600-mile road march from Ft. Benning to Panama City, Florida and back. The spectacle of the division's then 6,500 men and 1,200 vehicles (175 tanks) rolling across the American southeast attracted nationwide media attention, and in small towns en route people lined the roads and schoolkids were released from classes to witness the march. The public had heard all the news about Germany's Panzer divisions, and for the first time got a glimpse of America's homegrown armored phalanx. Of course this, at the time, consisted mainly of Combat Cars, M2s and early M3 tanks.

In January 1941, over 2,000 new draftees came in, but the division lost just as many fully trained men as cadre for the newly forming 3rd and 4th Armored Divisions. During the spring the division held exercises along with the 4th Infantry Division and engaged in live-fire training. Gradually, 2AD's hodgepodge of equipment began to standardize with new halftracks, artillery, radios, and the M3 series of light and medium tanks.

No one is sure who invented the division's nickname, "Hell on Wheels," but during April and May of 1941 the phrase appeared repeatedly in Columbus, GA, newspaper articles and in Ft. Benning's newsletter. The name stuck (and prompted the 1st Armored Division commander to find a nickname of his own, which was voted in as "Old Ironsides"). The U.S. Army then set up a series of wide-scale exercises, to test the proficiency of its new divisions.

MANEUVERS

Patton's one and only divisional command took shape rapidly under his stern tutelage. He expected the men of the 2nd Armored not only to know their jobs as soldiers, but to look and act like soldiers, with firm discipline and strict dress codes. He earned his nickname, "Ol' Blood and Guts," during this period (far before the revise in the ETO, "Our blood and his guts") for inspirational speeches he gave to the troops in which he repeatedly invoked the phrase. The "Hell on Wheels" under its flamboyant commander was unveiled to the American brass and national public at the multi-divisional Tennessee Maneuvers in June 1941. This series of wargames took place on the old Civil War stomping grounds between Nashville and Chattanooga, and the participation of the 2nd Armored was much anticipated. The division rolled from Ft. Benning to Camp Forrest, Tennessee, and then Patton sent its components to secret locations for the kick-off of the games on June 19.

The 2nd Armored, as part of the Red force, got off to a tentative start on its first day of maneuvers. The 67th Armored Regiment ran into cleverly placed anti-tank concentrations, and umpires ruled the division had lost 135 tanks and suffered heavy casualties. By the end of the simulation the 2nd had bulldozed its way to its objectives and cornered Blue infantry, but was also about to suffer a flank counterattack from Blue armor. The first day ended in a draw.

The performance — and some resulting criticism — lit a flame under Patton and in the following simulations the 2nd Armored could not be stopped. In the next exercise, 67th Regiment tankers cut through opposing lines and captured the headquarters of the 5th Infantry Division, forcing umpires to call a halt. Now part of Blue, in the following simulation the 66th Armored flanked the opposing Red force on the east while the 82nd

Below: M2A4 Light Tanks of Company H, 66th Armored Regiment, at Saturday inspection, Fort Benning, May 1941. Not to be confused with the M2 medium seen on page 7, the M2 Light Tank derived from the earlier Combat Cars M1 and M2. The principal M2 production type was the M2A4 which boasted two .30 MGs in side sponsons as well as the 37mm and coaxial .30 MG in the turret. The M2 Light Tank saw some action in the Pacific Theater. *via Chris Ellis*

Armored Reconnaissance Battalion, with elements of the 41st Armored Infantry and 78th Armored Artillery, cut through from the west. The hammerblow came when the rest of the 2nd Armored Brigade attacked head-on. Umpires had to stop the exercise just 40 minutes after the main attack had begun.

In the final simulation the 2nd Armored and the 5th Infantry Division were ordered to stage an offensive against the town of Tullahoma. In keeping with Patton's philosophy, "Hold 'em by the nose and kick 'em in the pants," 5th Division demonstrated along the opposing front while the 2nd Armored crossed the Duck River to sweep around the flanks. After six hours, far earlier than expected, Tullahoma had fallen to the tankers.

On July 7, 1941, *Life* magazine featured General Patton on its cover, standing upright in the turret of a tank, a 2AD patch above his left breast, a pistol in a shoulder holster, and a fierce look on his face. Six months prior to Pearl Harbor a hero had already been found, and to the public, "Hell on Wheels" had become America's premier armored division — America's own answer to Blitzkrieg.

The Louisiana Maneuvers took place six weeks later. The largest yet, involving over 350,000 troops, tens of thousands of vehicles and hundreds of aircraft, they were intended to weed out inept commanders or identify new talent. The maneuvers were a nightmare to the troops, who were confronted with bayous, lakes and rivers on every side, as well as chiggers, snakes and Deep South humidity. Nevertheless the 2nd Armored again ran roughshod over opponents, its engineers and reconnaissance paving the way for surprise concentrations of firepower. At one point the 1st Armored Division happened onto the rear of the 2nd Armored while it was preparing for an attack and the two divisions slugged it out. But then umpires arrived on the scene and realized that the two divisions were supposed to have been in separate exercises.

The highlight of the maneuvers featured the Red Second Army, built around the I Armored Corps, taking on a far larger, infantry-heavy Blue Third Army. The tactical objectives for each side were the bridges and few hard roads in the area. Though 2AD's 41st Armored Infantry got behind the opposing lines and created havoc, 2nd Armored's tanks got held up by swamps, whereupon they fell to hunter-killer anti-tank teams. The Blue 1st Cavalry slipped through Red lines and captured the 2nd Armored's gasoline supplies, completely immobilizing the tank regiments and ending the exercise. The 2nd Armored had been bested for the first time, albeit on unholy terrain while pitted against superior numbers.

The Carolina maneuvers followed in the fall, and with solid ground again under its feet, the 2nd Armored resumed running over its opposition. In these simulations the division practiced with new police-type radios, which allowed voice communications between tanks instead of Morse code. In the final simulation the I Armored Corps, launched a massive attack, but the 1st Armored and 4th Infantry Divisions (Motorized) were stopped. The 2nd Armored had to act as rearguard in a corps withdrawal.

The Carolina maneuvers ended on November 28, and after four months in the field, the 2nd Armored Division returned to Fort Benning. Barely a week later, Japan attacked Pearl Harbor. Within days, the U.S.A. was at war with Germany, too. Hell on Wheels had already established an unsurpassed reputation in maneuvers, but now it would have to prove itself in the real thing.

> ## "Hell on Wheels"
> The 2nd Armored Division is said to have received its nickname during the maneuvers in Tennessee, Louisiana, when the division rode roughshod over all the other outfits.

Below: M2 and M3 halftracks exercising at Fort Benning in July 1942. The M2 gun tower and M3 personnel carrier were the mainstays of U.S. armored units during the war. Produced in huge numbers, they were developed as mortar carriers, gun and howitzer motor carriages, as well carrying many forms of mobile AAA — from twin .50 cals to the experimental T68 with two 40mm guns. *Via Chris Ellis*

READY FOR WAR

After Pearl Harbor, America began mobilizing in earnest, somewhat to the disadvantage of the 2nd Armored Division, which lost many of its trained men as cadre to newly forming divisions, replacement centers and officer training schools. On January 18, 1942 the division also lost its general when Patton was promoted to command of the I Armor Corps. Patton had planned to vacate his post without ceremony, but the men caught word of his departure and lined the streets with cheers and salutes when he rode through the bivouac. Brigadier General Willis D. Crittenberger, an energetic, hands-on commander, was assigned to take his place.

The Army reorganized at this juncture, eliminating armored regiments designated light or medium. Instead, each regiment would contain two battalions of medium tanks and one of lights. The 68th Regiment (Light) was disbanded, its men and equipment dispersed among the division. A shift in nomenclature also took place so that, aside from dropping the light or medium designations from tank regiments, the division's infantry, artillery, reconnaissance, engineers and other units would henceforth have the word "armored" following their numerals. Thus, for example, the 41st Infantry (Armored) became the 41st Armored Infantry.

Above: An M2A4 light tank at Fort Benning in 1941. Note the sponson-mounted .30-cal machine guns, riveted construction and early-style tanker's helmet. *Courtesy of Mark Bando*

The Army had also decided that the armored brigade system was too unwieldy to command in the field, so it switched to a system of combat commands, each built around a tank regiment. This flexible system was as if the divisional command group acted as a head, wielding two arms, Combat Commands A and B, either of which could be the primary haymaker, reinforced with divisional artillery or armored infantry as the situation required. In addition to CCA and CCB, the command group, holding back elements, could thrust a third arm into the battlefield as CCR, Combat Command Reserve.

The 2nd Armored suffered more attrition in trained personnel when it was ordered to provide men and equipment — mainly M7 105mm SP guns — to form the independent 702nd Tank Destroyer Battalion. However, the 702nd TD would be attached to the "Hell on Wheels" through most of the war and be considered an integral part of the division.

As the 2nd Armored intensified its training and tried to absorb thousands of replacements, the war news in early 1942 was dismal. The Germans had crushed a huge Soviet counteroffensive at Kharkov, and were on their way to obliterating Soviet forces in the Crimea. As summer began the Germans launched a gigantic offensive toward the Soviet oilfields in the south. In the Pacific, both the American Philippines and the British Malaysian peninsula had fallen to Japanese arms, the latter defeat also giving up some 130,000 prisoners. Things were no better in North Africa where General Erwin Rommel's Afrika Korps flanked the British Gazala Line with a deep hook through the desert. As the

2ND ARMORED UNITS
as at January 8, 1942

HQ & HQ Co
CCA and CCB
Division Service Co
142nd Signal Co (formerly 48th)
Division Artillery
14th Armored Fd Arty
78th Armored Fd Arty
92nd Armored Fd Arty
Div Trains & HQ Co
48th Armd Med Bn
2nd Armd Maint Bn (formerly
    17th Ordnance Bn)
2nd Armd Supply (formerly 14th QM
    Bn)
17th Engineer Bn
41st Inf. Regt
66th Armd Regt
67th Armd Regt
82nd Recon Bn

British front crumbled, the Germans rushed on to capture Tobruk and 30,000 men. During the spring, U-boats had arrived off the American coast for a hunting spree that German captains later termed the "happy time." Scores of Allied cargo vessels and tankers went down in sight of the shores of New York, New Jersey and Florida.

That summer the 2nd Armored was stripped of its tanks, which were put aboard ship and dispatched under heavy convoy guard to reinforce the British Eighth Army in Africa. Selected 2AD men accompanied the vehicles to oversee their maintenance. Some also got a taste of combat. One man, Sergeant John Dinan of the 66th Armored, participated in a battle with the Afrika Korps, in which his unit lost 10 of its 12 tanks. General Charles Scott, the 2nd Armored's first commander, was sent to North Africa to report on the fighting. He said that the Germans pulled the British onto anti-tank screens while Rommel husbanded his own armor for flank attacks. According to Scott, the British had little sense for coordinating armor, air and artillery, and their tanks, on encountering the enemy, would invariably stop to fire. Generally outranged by German guns, the British tanks would then brew up while the enemy counterattacked. He recommended that U.S. tactics emphasize the combination of fire with movement, involving all arms.

On July 31, 1942, Crittenberger was promoted to command the III Armored Corps and Brig. General Ernest Harmon stepped up to lead the 2nd Armored. A short, stocky officer given to profanity, "Old Gravel Voice" Harmon would prove to be one of the outstanding combat commanders of the war.

As the last of the great powers to enter World War II, the United States held an advantage in that it fielded a proper main battle tank from the start — the M4 Sherman. Other powers had begun the war with the equivalent of the M2 Combat Car, but these were soon wiped from the battlefield. America's first good medium tank, the M3 Lee (or, as the British called it, the Grant), was overtaken by the Sherman in 1942.

Into the late 1930s, tank designers had trouble reconciling a large gun with a revolving turret, so the M3 medium contained a 75mm gun with very limited traverse in a sponson on the right side of its hull and a 37mm gun up top in the turret. This was essentially the same design as the best French tank in 1940, the Char B. But the concept — a combination of motorized artillery and weak tank power — became obsolete once engineers on all sides had surmounted the turret problem. The Lee/Grant was a sturdy vehicle, and thanks to American largesse Montgomery fielded over 200 of them at El Alamein. Its successor, the M4 Sherman, several tons heavier but with the same 25mph speed and featuring a 75mm gun in its turret, was far better. The Sherman first emerged in September 1941 and those that made it to North Africa by the summer of 1942 were rated the best tank in the desert, superior to the German Mark IV. Montgomery had almost 300 at Alamein.

Having gained from the observation of previous combats, the Americans thus entered the war with a tank that would have swept clean the battlefields of 1939–41. The Sherman went into full production, between one and two thousand a month, and by the end of the war over 50,000 had been produced — double the number of German tanks of all types. The Germans had begun the war with a series of types, which ranged from the Mark I, mounting machine guns, to the Mark IV, their "heavy" in 1939–41, which was constantly upgraded so that later models featured long 75mm guns. The advantage was that each tank in the series shared enough design components so that assembly lines could be adapted to newer models — when the Mark III became obsolete, its chassis was quickly adopted for use in assault guns.

The primary American light tank was the M3 Stuart, called Honey by the British. It mounted a 37mm main gun plus machine guns and eventually had a decent 55mm of frontal armor. Once it was fitted with twin Cadillac V-8 engines in 1942 (and redesignated the M5), it was able to reach a speed of nearly 40mph, making it the most mobile piece of armor on the battlefield. Though it needed to avoid enemy armor or anti-tank guns, it was invaluable in reconnaissance and breakthrough operations, as per its cavalryman namesake. About a third of tanks in U.S. armored divisions were lights, with the main strength depending on the rugged, reliable, more powerful Sherman M4.

The only problem with the Sherman was that while it indeed trumped earlier WWII tanks and could hold its own with the Mark IV, the Germans had been shocked by the Soviets into another leap in tank technology. In late 1941 the Germans had encountered the Russian T-34, a superb, if crude, medium tank, and then the KV-1, a goliath that was almost impossible to knock out. German designers rushed to their drawing boards, with the result that while the U.S. entered the conflict with a tank that could defeat the machines of 1941, the German (and Soviet) tanks of 1943–45 were in a different class. Germany's new heavy was called the Tiger, and its new medium the Panther. Though German industrial capacity did not allow for fully arming their Panzer divisions with these "zoo" machines, the 2nd Armored would encounter both animals often enough in the war to come. And both could easily kill a Sherman.

By mid-summer 1942, American troops had still not confronted the Germans, and the pressure from both the British government and U.S. Chief of Staff George Marshall to engage the enemy had become acute. The Americans were convinced that a direct attack on France would be the quickest way to end the war. The more experienced British lobbied for U.S. participation in their North African campaign. While Marshall pressed hard for an early cross-Channel attack, which surely would have been a fiasco, the British launched one of their own on August 17, 1942. This division-sized raiding force was crushed by the Germans on the beaches of Dieppe, about half the men able to retreat to England. It was decided that America's first invasion would be aimed at North Africa.

The joint U.S.–British invasion, Operation Torch, called for accelerated maneuvers to disembark men and equipment on hostile shores. On the evening of October 10, the men of 2nd Armored's CCB practiced an amphibious landing with sailors from the operation's task force. The exercise took place on a stretch of beaches along Chesapeake Bay, with a beaming lighthouse to help guide the landing craft ashore. It turned into chaos. The only boat that reached its target was General Harmon's own — and he was supposed to be in the third wave. All the other landing craft were scattered along the Maryland coast and it took until the following afternoon to assemble the troops. Harmon was depressed and deeply worried about how 2AD would achieve the same task under fire. Other U.S. officers were equally concerned about how inexperienced U.S. troops would perform in Operation Torch. Or as Patton floridly described it to his brother-in-law, "As desperate a venture as has ever been undertaken by any force in the world's history."

Below: 4th Infantry Division troops pass an M3 Grant of the 2nd Armored Division at Fort Benning in February 1942. Note the sponson-mounted 75mm main gun. In spite of its limited traverse, its dual-purpose — HE or AP — capability proved a major asset. Transferred in large quantities to the British, who called it the Grant, the M3 medium proved to be a good match for the Panzers of the Afrika Korps in the desert in the summer of 1942. *Via Chris Ellis*

IN ACTION

Operation Torch consisted of three major amphibious invasions of North African territory held by Vichy France. Preceded by a strong Royal Navy armada to ward off Axis naval interference, two transport fleets sailed from the British Isles through the straits of Gibraltar into the Mediterranean. The Eastern Task Force, primarily British, landed at Algiers, while the American Central Task Force, spearheaded by the 1st Armored and 1st Infantry Divisions and Darby's Rangers, landed around the city of Oran.

The Western Task Force, including the 2nd Armored Division, sailed across the Atlantic from the United States to invade a 200-mile stretch of the Atlantic coast of Morocco centered on Casablanca. Under the overall command of George Patton, the assault forces of the Western Task Force were divided into three elements. Farthest south, Operation Blackstone was commanded by Ernest Harmon, who had Combat Command B of his 2AD and the 47th Infantry Regimental Combat Team (RCT) of the 9th Infantry. His objective was the port of Safi, 140 miles southwest of Casablanca. Operation Brushwood would land troops at Fedala near the capital and was led by Major General Jonathan Anderson with his 3rd Infantry Division and a combat team from the 1st Battalion, 67th Armored Regiment. Sixty miles northeast of Casablanca, Major General Lucian Truscott, Jr. commanded Operation Goalpost, targeting Port Lyautey and its nearby airfield with an RCT of his 9th Infantry Division and the 1st Battalion, 66th Armored.

At Safi, the invasion began just after midnight on November 8 with 47th Infantry scouts dispatched from a U.S. submarine. With blackened faces, the men rowed rubber boats into the harbor where they were to set up infrared lanterns to guide in two destroyers, the *Cole* and *Bernadou*, packed with infantrymen. But as with most aspects of the invasion, the carefully formulated plans went awry.

The scouts were spotted by French sentries and had to take cover. A Navy ensign was sent in as machine-gun fire crisscrossed the docks. The *Bernadou* came slowly into port around 4:30 a.m., and

Below: U.S. Army tank crews load ammunition aboard M4s just landed in Algeria. The M4 could carry between 90 and 100 rounds of 75mm ammunition and nearly 5,000 rounds of .30 cal for its hull-mounted and coaxial machine guns. *Via Chris Ellis*

then the French opened up with artillery fire from the town and from 155mm batteries on surrounding cliffs. Suddenly the ship ran onto a sandbar, jolting the soldiers in its hold, who were terrified enough at the ordnance pounding against the hull. The infantry clambered over the sides of the ship and hastily waded ashore.

As soon as the French had opened fire, the signal "Play ball!" had been dispatched to the fleet, and the battleship *New York* and cruiser *Philadelphia* took on the French 155mm battery, guided by its gun flashes. The second U.S. destroyer, *Cole*, came veering into the harbor, barely missing a concrete jetty, and unloaded its cargo of infantry. A huge transport ship, the *Dix* — carrying 1,450 men and 1,500 tons of vehicles — suffered an accidental explosion while trying to unload a truck. Ammo started going off and the men on board thought they had been torpedoed. The *Dix*'s pyrotechnics lit up the night until it finally sank in shallow water.

Harmon was soon out of contact with his landing force. With full daylight he couldn't restrain himself and went ashore to see what was going on. Eight or 10 Stuarts had gotten ashore via lighters during the night, but they were inoperable, their batteries waterlogged. However, by now the Americans controlled the harbor, and the former Caribbean seatrain, *Lakehurst*, carrying the 2nd Armored's medium tanks, and the *Titania*, filled with lights, pulled in. Unfortunately, a crane on the *Lakehurst* malfunctioned while it was lifting a tank and remained frozen in place for five hours. On the *Titania*, a cable snapped when it was trying to unload a Stuart, and that took even longer to fix.

On shore, a frustrated Harmon kicked some stalled infantrymen into action and went back to his command ship. There he was handed an intelligence report that a French force of 70 trucks and 1,000 infantry was headed for Safi from Marrakech, 90 miles inland. Since ship-to-ship radios (unlike the land ones) were operable, he was able to dispatch orders to the aircraft carrier *Santee* to fend them off. Navy Wildcats bombed and strafed the column until 36 trucks were burning on the road and the French had retreated.

Returning to the beachhead, Harmon found that some of his tanks were finally available but his force was still under sniper fire. Some of it appeared to be coming from a nearby house, but twice it was investigated and the troops reported there was no one inside but an old man and woman. When fire again erupted from the house, Harmon told a tank commander to roll up to the front door and blast the place down. This accomplished, some 30 French soldiers emerged from a hidden basement. The man and woman were found dead in the rubble.

Despite his aggravations, at least Harmon had calm seas. In the north at Port Lyautey, Truscott's landing craft were being dashed against rocks and jetties by high waves. Fire from French coastal batteries — alerted by a broadcast from President Roosevelt announcing the invasion — added to the confusion. Somehow the first wave of assault boats got lost and the second wave landed first. Radios had already failed and now Truscott's landing force was emerging from the surf with soaked equipment, the vehicles with drenched engines. A hilltop fortification called the Casbah, manned by some 250 French, was holding out against all attacks. U.S. infantry companies had been scattered across five miles of shore, officers were missing, and many of the infantrymen had shrunk from their first taste of fire. Unable to coordinate, or even find, most of his command, as Truscott sat down in the middle of his beachhead in the early morning hours of November 9, he learned that a powerful French column led by at least 15 tanks was on its way to counterattack.

Fortunately, Lt. Colonel Harry Semmes of the attached 2nd Armored combat team was nearby, and was guided to the general for instructions. Truscott told him to take his seven operational tanks to a crossroads to intercept the attack. At dawn the French tanks found Semmes' contingent of the "Hell on Wheels" waiting for them. Four Renaults were knocked out in short order when the Stuarts opened fire. The tanks swept the surrounding

Above: The Operation Torch landings saw American ground forces enter the war against Germany. This is a rare scene from where things went smoothly on the beaches of French Morocco. Elsewhere the U.S. Army found it had much to learn about amphibious logistics and command coordination.
U.S. Army via George Forty

Above: A Sherman in action at El Guettar. Note the three-piece bolted nose section that identifies the early production vehicles; later production models had a one-piece cast hull. *Via Chris Ellis*

field with machine-gun fire, keeping the infantry at bay. The French retreated to a wooded area, whereupon a spotter plane dispatched their coordinates to Navy warships. The woods were plastered with heavy ordnance and the French withdrew.

After the battle Semmes, who had accounted for two of the enemy Renaults, dismounted from his tank, casually lit a cigarette, and saw that two French 37mm shells were embedded in his front armor. Patton received a report on Operation Goalpost that day and jotted in his diary, "Truscott has Lyautey but not the airport. Had a tank fight with 15 Renaults. Semmes must have had a good time."

At Fedala, in the center of the invasion zone, the 3rd Infantry Division and its 2AD tanks also suffered from heavy waves, rocky shores and nocturnal confusion. Of 116 assault boats, 62 were wrecked after crashlanding on the rocks. But ground resistance was light and the main action in Operation Broadwood was naval as the French fleet sallied out from Casablanca. Around 8:00 five destroyers and a light cruiser emerged from a heavy smokescreen to take on the American fleet. The battleship *Jean Bart*, moored in Casablanca harbor, added salvoes from its 15-inch guns. French coastal batteries opened up while Navy Wildcats dived on the *Jean Bart*, the coastal guns and warships. French Dewoitine fighters raced to the battle from inland to fend off the Wildcats.

The French ships dodged skillfully in and out of their smokescreen to inflict damage on the destroyers *Ludlow* and *Wilkes*. But the heavier guns of the cruisers *Brooklyn* and *Augusta* forced them back into the harbor. At 9:30 they sallied again, and the American warships once more formed a shield between the French and the vulnerable U.S. transport fleet. After an hour-long slugfest the French flagship, *Milan*, was burning aground, two other destroyers were sunk, and the cruiser *Primauguet* was chased down by U.S. aircraft and set afire. The stationary *Jean Bart* had already become a smoking ruin in Casablanca harbor.

Back at Safi, the tanks of 2nd Armored's CCB had finally been unloaded, and though new French counterattacks were emerging from the south, Harmon decided to follow the original plan to swing his command north toward Casablanca, leaving the 9th Infantry RCT to hold the port. This was a large gamble because CCB had no means of carrying extra fuel, and the only hope of resupply was from a U.S. destroyer that was supposed to arrive at Mazagan, 90 miles to the north. After dark on November 9, the 2AD column plunged into the unknown, its men keeping careful march discipline due to reports that knife-wielding Arab Bedouins were lurking in the dark to pounce on stragglers.

At dawn the column arrived to take Mazagan without a fight, and the destroyer had indeed arrived with fuel. After a further 40 miles, CCB was south of Casablanca, which was still holding out against the American invasion.

As it appeared on November 10, the other aspects of Operation Torch had gone well. Algiers had fallen quickly, and the defenses of Oran, after some extremely heavy fighting, were about to crumble. At Port Lyautey in Morocco, Truscott had reduced the Casbah at the cost of 225 casualties. At the end, fighter-bombers and point-blank artillery fire had forced the French to surrender.

From his cramped headquarters dug into the rock of Gibraltar, Allied commander Dwight Eisenhower got a message to Patton, saying that Casablanca was the last of the great nuts to crack. Patton wondered if Ike's message was a rebuke, but in any case he was now in position to raze the place to the ground. Now that Harmon was south of the city, Anderson's 3rd Infantry was established to the north, dozens of P-40 Tomahawk aircraft had settled into Port Lyautey airfield, and with naval firepower and naval air poised offshore, an all-out assault on the city was planned for the next morning. Patton, perhaps reflecting that November 11 was not only Armistice Day but his own birthday, rescheduled the assault for 7:30, full daylight, instead of at dawn. At 6:40 in the morning, the French capitulated. Given the poor U.S. radio net there was a mad scramble to inform all units, but the attack was successfully called off. French officers sailed out to Patton's command ship, the *Augusta*, for the official surrender. "They drank $37 of my wine," Patton complained afterward, "but it was worth it." That day, all French resistance to the Anglo-American invasion ceased. That night, however, German U-boats slipped among the U.S. fleet off Casablanca and torpedoed five transport ships. In the Mediterranean, Luftwaffe aircraft destroyed half of a British convoy heading east from Algiers toward Tunisia.

In Berlin, once the Allied invasion had revealed itself, the German high command reacted quickly. First, the remainder of mainland France was overrun so that the Germans could guard the Mediterranean coast. Vichy France ceased to exist. Second, the Germans immediately began pouring troops, tanks and equipment into Tunisia, which at its closest point was just 90 miles from Sicily. Strategically, the Allied gamble had been to crush Rommel's Afrika Korps in a vice. Now the German gamble was to reinforce North Africa, so that not only Britain's army could be tied down in that theater for the foreseeable future, but the American one as well. Operation Torch turned into a race for Tunisia.

Outside Tunis, east of ancient Carthage, the Germans negotiated with Vichy French officers not to oppose their air landings. They had soon poured 15,000 men into their bridgehead, along with weapons including their new Tiger tanks. General Jürgen von Arnim was transferred from Russia to command this force, Fifth Panzer Army. The initial Allied stab for Tunisia, led by British general Kenneth Anderson, was repulsed. At the close of 1942 Rommel's Afrika Korps began arriving in the area after its long retreat from Egypt. Now two Axis armies were concentrated, and the Allies looked forward to a harsh North African winter in difficult, mountainous terrain.

Through the winter of 1942–43 the Allied front became strung out for 200 miles due-south from the coast, the British in the north, the Americans in the south, and an improvised Free French army in between. When Rommel pulled up to this position, followed by Montgomery's Eighth Army, he assessed that a blow against the neophyte Americans would provide the best breathing room. On Valentine's Day 1943 he and von Arnim coordinated a Panzer strike west, cutting a bloody swathe through the U.S. 1st Armored Division. The American front was pushed back almost 40 miles to the Kasserine Pass. The U.S. lost over 6,000 men to the German offensive, half of them captured. But the extent of the debacle was not reflected in the casualties as much as by troops retreating in disorder, abandoning their equipment. The Germans were astonished and often delighted at the wealth of material they inherited, including working vehicles, weapons, stocks of gasoline and rations.

Above: After the U.S. defeat at Kasserine, the 2nd Armored was asked to lend much of its equipment to the 1st Armored Division. This 82nd Recon Battalion halftrack subsequently met a bad end in the North African desert. *Courtesy of Mark Bando*

Below: The campaign in North Africa.

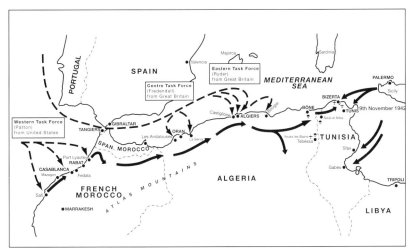

Above: American armor moves into battle in Tunisia. U.S. M4 mediums enter the valley of El Guettar during the battle of Bir Marbott Pass, which the Americans captured from the Axis, forcing them to retreat down the road to Gabes. *U.S. Army via Chris Ellis*

Right: M4A1s in Sicily. Note the smooth cast hull that identifies this version of the tank, the first to go into production. *U.S. Army via George Forty*

The Kasserine battle was the first American crisis in the European war, and the 2nd Armored was deeply affected. First it lost its divisional commander, Harmon, who flew east to direct the battle and eventually to assume command of the battered 1st Armored Division. Then the 2AD lost its corps commander, Patton, who took temporary command of U.S. II Corps in Tunisia. Finally, each tank company of the "Hell on Wheels" in Morocco was requested to provide the equivalent of one platoon to make good the losses in the 1st Armored. Naturally, company commanders took this opportunity to get rid of all their slackers and malcontents, although one captain provided an entire platoon, his 3rd, intact. The 2nd Armored was also called upon to provide equipment to form the 2nd French Armored Division, a unit created more for political than military reasons.

As a final consequence of Kasserine, the British chiefs maneuvered to elevate their Allied supreme commander, Dwight Eisenhower, into "the stratosphere," to remove him from control of operations and to place the British officers Alexander (land forces), Tedder (air) and Cunningham (naval) as his immediate subordinates. This put the Americans, whom some British troops had begun to call "our Italians," out of harm's way so that proper operations could be conducted in the future. Naturally, Ike's sidelining by the British was resented by other U.S. officers, especially men like Patton, Bradley and Harmon.

At the end of 1942 there were suggestions to transfer the 2nd Armored from Morocco to the battlefront in Tunisia. But logistics there were weak, and there was a remaining strategic concern in Morocco. The greatest trump the Germans could still play in the Mediterranean would be persuading Franco's Fascist Spain to join the Axis, or at least to bend its neutrality to allow German divisions to cross its territory. At one stroke, this could have closed the Gibraltar strait, effectively trapping Allied forces in the Mediterranean. Opposite Gibraltar sat Spanish Morocco with 130,000 of Franco's troops. Maintaining the U.S. 2nd Armored Division in French Morocco was a powerful influence on the Spanish not to jump into the war.

As the winter of 1942–43 progressed — including news of the German disaster at Stalingrad and the huge Allied build-up in North Africa — fears of Spanish intervention, perhaps planted by German Intelligence in the first place, receded. By then the 2nd Armored had been largely cannibalized for men and equipment. But in the following months the rest of the division and enough replacements made it across the Atlantic to restore a first-class fighting force. Harmon was replaced as divisional commander by Brig. Gen. Allen Kingman, but Kingman's French language skills and specialized expertise were soon needed elsewhere. Hugh Gaffey, who had formerly commanded 2nd Armored's CCB and more recently had been Patton's II Corps chief of staff, assumed command in May. In the spring of 1943, 2AD practiced amphibious landings along the North African coast. Borrowing (or retrieving) a great deal of equipment from the 1st Armored Division, the 2nd Armored prepared for the next jump in the Allies' Mediterranean strategy.

OPERATION HUSKY

The Allied invasion of Sicily was commanded by British General Harold Alexander's 15th Army Group, consisting of Montgomery's Eighth Army and Patton's new Seventh Army. Formerly U.S. I Corps with attachments from II Corps, Seventh Army was activated at sea en route to the beaches. With 180,000 men, Husky was the largest seaborne invasion in history to that time, and still ranks second only to Normandy. Eisenhower, as commander-in-chief of Allied forces, established his headquarters in Malta where he could oversee all ground, air and naval actions.

An early plan for the invasion had called for the Americans to assault the west of the island, near Palermo, while the British attacked the southeast around Syracuse. The two German commanders in Sicily seemed to anticipate this contingency by deploying the 15th Panzer Grenadier Division in the west and the *Hermann Göring* Panzer Division in the center-southeast. Instead, Seventh Army was assigned to hit a 70-mile stretch of coastline in the south, to the left of the British landings. The key city in Sicily was Messina in the northeast corner, separated from the Italian mainland only by a tiny strait that the ancient Greeks thought was guarded by the monsters Scylla and Charybdis, but which today is known as the Strait of Messina.

As the only U.S. armored division in the invasion, the 2nd Armored was split between two of the three Seventh Army task forces. On the left, Combat Command A accompanied the 3rd Division (now led by Lucian Truscott) in landings at Licata, the whole known as Joss Force. The bulk of the division was employed as a floating reserve to support the central invasion around Gela. The third task force, closest to the the British, was targeted on the village of Scoglitti.

The invasion commenced just after midnight on July 10, 1943, with attacks by the American 82nd Airborne and British 6th Airborne Divisions. These turned into a fiasco as the 82nd's paratroopers were scattered all over the landscape, hardly anyone hitting their drop zones. It was worse for the British glider force, which was released in the dark into heavy headwinds, most of the craft crashing into the sea.

At dawn, the 2,590 ships of the Allied armada were revealed offshore and the Italian coastal divisions turned out to have no stomach for a fight. Italian artillery inland fired on the beaches and the coastal troops unleashed occasional rounds, but the general picture was Italian troops surrendering quickly, sometimes after firing a few shots for "honor". The coastal divisions largely consisted of Sicilian conscripts who had not been enthusiastic about Mussolini and the war in the first place, especially after all the disasters in North Africa.

Meanwhile, since the Allies had ignored the western half of the island, the 15th Panzer Grenadiers were ordered to move east from their positions near Palermo and the *Hermann Göring* Panzer Division immediately launched a counterattack on the American beachhead at Gela.

On the first day the *HG* Panzers, coordinating with the Italian *Livorno* Division and Mobile Force E, got off to a late start. The Luftwaffe armored division was not then an experienced force and suffered from some incompetent officers. It had a capable General in Paul Conrath, however, and after the division initially stalled, Conrath relieved one of his regimental commanders and personally went to the front. By the end of the day his infantry and tanks had overrun a battalion of the U.S. 45th Division, capturing its commander. On the right, Italy's Mobile Force E got into Gela town to meet vicious resistance from Darby's Rangers. The Italian tanks ranged from 10 tons to three tons (about the weight of a Buick), and many were destroyed by Rangers throwing grenades or demolition charges from second-story windows. The German force was split into two columns: infantry backed by Tigers on the left and a greater number of medium Panzers in the center.

The call went out for 2nd Armored, Seventh Army's floating reserve, to get some tanks on shore. Col. Isaac White disembarked in late

Above: Irvine Lafleur of the 17th Armored Engineer
Battalion strikes a contemplative pose while on
occupation duty in Palermo, Sicily, 1943.
Courtesy of Mark Bando

afternoon to set up an assembly area and by midnight was joined by the rest of CCB's personnel. With Luftwaffe bombers attacking the transports, everyone was anxious to get off the ships. But due to confusion in the fleet and high waves, only two platoons of Shermans were unloaded, and these bogged down on the beach. The Navy decided to wait for daylight before resuming operations.

On the morning of July 11, the *Hermann Göring* Panzers came in again, supported by the *Livorno* Division. The Italians ran into another buzzsaw and were knocked out of the fight. On the left, the Germans were held up by a heroic stand of 82nd Paratroopers and mixed units under Col. James Gavin on Biazza Ridge. But the German righthand column forced the greatest crisis of the day.

In the center, some 40 German Mark IIIs and Mark IVs crashed through the lines of the 1st Infantry Division, overrunning several companies. Having pierced the U.S. perimeter they now had only to cross an open plain to the beaches. This flat area was bisected by a tree-lined coastal highway. Behind that highway, every American artillery piece, infantry mortar or small-arm within range fired into the approaching Panzers. The Navy cruisers *Boise* and *Savannah* joined in with 5- and 8-inch shells.

General Patton came ashore that afternoon, walking backwards with a movie camera to record his own arrival. Then he dropped the camera and repeated the maneuver frontways for the benefit of the assembled press. At the time, 2nd Armored's tanks were having a difficult time getting off the beach. Chicken wire had been spread on the sand to provide traction, but it became tangled up in the treads, clogging the sprockets. Some tanks chose the soft sand instead and threw their tracks.

Out on the Gela plain, U.S. artillerymen had leveled their pieces and were now firing over open sights against the German armor. Urgent word had gotten back to the beaches and four 2nd Armored Shermans led by Lt. James White finally made it out of the sand to take position along the coastal highway. These started pouring shells into the German flank. Other men from 82nd Recon came rushing up on foot to add small-arms fire. With the torrent of explosions around them, the Panzers were slow to realize that Shermans were hitting them from the right. Then the Panzers traversed and all the dismounted men ducked for cover, the Shermans continuing to fire.

At Col. White's CP, Major Clifton Batchelder of the 3rd Battalion, 67th Armored, reported for orders and asked what the plan was. "Plans hell!" White yelled. "This may be Custer's last stand!" But by now the Germans had had enough. The two Panzer battalions withdrew, leaving 16 smoldering tanks on the plain. The dramatic siege at Biazza Ridge was broken shortly after when six Shermans came to Gavin's aid.

At Licata, the westernmost U.S. beachhead, Maurice Rose's 2nd Armored CCA, which had practiced amphibious landings with the 3rd Infantry Division, got its tanks ashore more easily, beginning on July 10. The next day, however, the Luftwaffe destroyed an LST carrying a company of Shermans, vehicles for an infantry company, and half of CCA's headquarters equipment. Early in the morning of that day, Col. Sidney Hinds led a column inland to seize Naro, the first Sicilian town captured by 2AD, but after the town was secured a squadron of B-26 Mitchells flew in and bombed it. The Sicilian campaign was characterized by uncoordinated air support — during the crisis at Gela Allied planes had not shown up at all — and by the end of the campaign 2nd Armored had suffered more casualties from mistaken U.S. air attacks than from the Luftwaffe.

As the *Hermann Göring* Panzer Division withdrew inland, the 2nd Armored spent several days taking villages and mopping up Italian resistance. The rocky hills of Sicily were difficult for armor and where the Italians chose to fight they could spring deadly ambushes with anti-tank guns. On balance, however, the Italians seemed hardly more eager for a fight than the Vichy French, though there were more of them. On July 16, the 2nd Armored was pulled into army reserve.

Now that they were established ashore, the Allies' further strategy was unclear. Montgomery was heading up the east coast toward Mount Etna and Messina, yet Patton and Bradley, who commanded II Corps, were refused the use of roads that would allow their own northern drive. Alexander visited the Seventh Army beachhead and it was seen that he didn't have a single American on his staff. In fact, he had had a poor opinion of the U.S. Army since Kasserine and thought it was incapable of mounting successful offensives against the Germans. His own idea was to use Eighth Army as the sword against the heart of the German position in Sicily (Messina) while Seventh Army would be the shield, protecting its left. Thus, Montgomery would win the campaign while the Americans essentially stood by in a defensive role. For various reasons Patton was already in hot water with Eisenhower and was momentarily unable to object openly to Alexander. He thus formulated his own plan. Denied the chance for a full-blooded drive north, he would instead attack west to seize Palermo, the capital of the island.

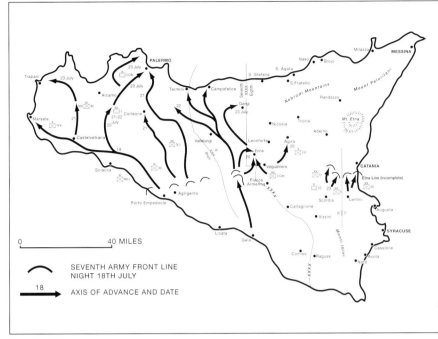

Above: Map of the Sicilian campaign — 2nd Armored's hottest action took place north of Gela, helping to fend off the *Hermann Göring* Division's counterattack.

To assault Palermo, Patton formed a provisional corps under his deputy, Geoffrey Keyes, consisting of the 2nd Armored, 3rd Infantry, 82nd Airborne, elements of the 9th Infantry, and two battalions of Darby's Rangers. Although this may sound like a veritable all-star line-up of U.S. units at this stage of the war, the provisional corps was aimed in the opposite direction to the true fighting in Sicily. The Germans had already vacated the northwest, devoting all their energy to setting up three successive defense lines to protect the northeast.

The attack of the Provisional Corps was spearheaded by the 3rd Infantry Division and two battalions of Rangers, with the 2nd Armored, providing transport for the 82nd Airborne, in reserve. The attack kicked off on July 20 and made fast progress through winding mountain roads. On July 22, B Company of the 82nd Recon sped into Palermo on reports that an Italian battleship was moored in its harbor. Col. Hinds, who led the advance party, seemed just as relieved when the ship turned out to have left the previous day. There was nothing in the Army instruction manuals to explain what he was to do if he found it.

Afterward there was some dispute whether patrols of the 2nd Armored or 3rd Infantry had been first to enter Palermo, but in a city of 400,000 it could have been both or either. For the official surrender, Keyes brought up the 2nd Armored for an impressive show of force through the streets. In the United States, Patton's plan was vindicated by huge headlines lauding the first Allied capture of a major Axis city. Though the operation had more publicity than strategic value, it enhanced the reputations of both "Hell on Wheels" and General Patton. The Provisional Corps suffered a total of 327 casualties in its drive on Palermo, out of some 21,500 Allied casualties in the Sicilian campaign as a whole.

Now fully enmeshed in Churchill's Mediterranean strategy, the Americans would next attack the ankle of the Italian mainland at Salerno, while the British attacked the foot at Taranto. For these operations the 1st Armored Division would resume the lead, and remain in that theater for the rest of the war. The 2nd Armored spent the next four months on occupation duty in Sicily.

While occupying Palermo, the 2nd Armored did not have a bad time. In order to confine "social diseases," or at least limit the disruptive effect of occupation on the civilian population, officers created "houses of joy," manned by 25 women at a time. In mid-September, Divisional Chaplain Urban J. Wurm became the most unpopular man in the 2AD when he persuaded General Gaffey to close down these facilities.

In a major misstep, the liberation of Sicily did produce a dire consequence. One success of Mussolini's Fascist regime had been to suppress the Sicilian Mafia. When the Americans took over they looked for community leaders who had not been connected with the dictator, and naturally dozens of Mafia leaders stepped forward. Palermo subsequently became a capital of organized crime, mobsters establishing themselves with wealth and power in a situation that the Italian government has struggled to control through the end of the century. It cannot be said that the U.S. was totally naive about the Mafia; prior to Operation Husky they had released Lucky Luciano from a New York state prison to help with intelligence.

In October, the 2nd Armored received orders to embark for England, leaving behind all its vehicles and heavy equipment. The division embarked on November 14, sailing far out into the Atlantic to evade the Luftwaffe and U-boats. Landing at Liverpool on Thanksgiving, the division moved into a former British cavalry post, Tidworth Barracks, on Salisbury Plain west of London. Over the next six months the 2nd Armored received new equipment and replacements while training for future amphibious operations. In March it gained a new commander in General Edward Brooks, an artillery specialist who had developed the M7 SP gun. For his new Third Army, Patton had wanted General Gaffey as his chief of staff.

At this time the U.S. general staff invoked a wholesale reorganization of armored divisions, switching from two tank regiments to three tank battalions, each supported by an independent battalion of armored infantry. This meant reducing the total strength of an armored division from over 14,000 men to about 10,500. With the invasion of France imminent, however, the first two armored divisions to land on the Continent, the 2nd Armored Division "Hell on Wheels" and the 3rd Armored, were exempted. They would remain organized as "heavy" armored divisions until the end of the war. Nevertheless, for the invasion, the 2nd Armored adjusted its force structure. Instead of the 66th and 67th Armored Regiments consisting of two medium tank battalions and one light, the types were integrated so that each battalion had both Shermans and Stuarts, on a two-to-one ratio.

In both Africa and Sicily, the 2nd Armored had vigorously executed all its assigned tasks. But it had often found itself too far to the west to participate in the decisive actions, fighting French and Italians rather than Germans. When the "Hell on Wheels" next hit enemy shores, however, it would relentlessly drive east against the Allies' primary opponents, all the way to Berlin.

Below: After a bitter week-long fight, 2nd Armored's Combat Command A fought its way into Tessy-sur-Vire, a key town on the vulnerable flank of Operation Cobra. On the date this picture was taken, August 3, 1944, the Germans were preparing a massive counterattack. *U.S. Army via Real War Photos*

NORMANDY

Operation Overlord, the invasion of France from England, began on June 6, 1944. Lead elements of the 2nd Armored Division boarded ships that day, but due to previous difficulties unloading mechanized units on hostile beaches, they were not included in the first wave. As it turned out, the 2AD was fortunate to have missed the initial landings. Two independent tank battalions, the 741st and 743rd, were assigned to support the assault troops on Omaha beach, their tanks modified with DD (duplex drive) equipment to "swim" ashore. The LSTs carrying the 741st Battalion released their tanks too early, into choppy seas 6,000 yards offshore, and 27 of 29 DD-tanks were swamped and sunk to the bottom. The 743rd Battalion was released closer in and most of its tanks made it to the beach, but by the next day half had been knocked out. On Omaha that day, tank support became a negligible factor as the looming cliffs were surmounted by the gallant efforts of the 1st and 29th Infantry Divisions.

The 2nd Armored began to disembark on Omaha Beach on June 9, by which time it had already suffered casualties. One LST transporting the division had hit a mine, losing 66 men, 31 tanks and 15 other heavy vehicles. Many men splashed into the water were recovered unwounded. In preparation for their arrival in the invasion, 2AD's tankers had waterproofed their tanks with heavy grease and affixed snorkel devices atop their rear compartments. When it came time to disembark, however, most of the vehicles were able to drive ashore barely dampening their treads. The division came ashore in three echelons: Combat Command A under Brig. General Maurice Rose, CCB under Brig. General Isaac White, with the supply train and other support units arriving last, when the landing schedules permitted.

The 2nd Armored was initially moved by First Army commander Omar Bradley to the American left. The 1st Infantry Division had advanced to Caumont, opening up a vulnerable eight-mile gap between the U.S. and British sectors. The 82nd Reconnaissance Battalion and regimental recon companies probed inland to contact neighboring units and get a feel for the enemy. After securing their seam with the British, the Americans spent the first week of the invasion fighting to connect their own two beachheads, Omaha and Utah, the area in between being dominated by the German-held town of Carentan. On June 12 the 101st Airborne Division seized the town, but then Omar Bradley learned through Ultra intercepts of German plans to counterattack with the 17th SS Panzer Grenadier Division, supported by the 6th Parachute Regiment. He ordered 2nd Armored to move a battalion each of tanks and armored infantry to the area. Rather than have to parcel out his command in small units, however, General

Above: During the Mortain counteroffensive, August 11, 1944, members of the 67th Armored Regiment examine a crater made by a German 105mm shell that landed five feet from their tank.
U.S. Army via Real War Photos

Right: On August 8, 1944, at the height of the Mortain counteroffensive, German POWs clear rubble from the streets of Barenton, watched by one of the division's MPs. *U.S. Army via Real War Photos*

Below right: During the first stages of Operation Cobra, on July 27, 1944, a group of the 2nd Armored's 17th Armored Engineer Battalion work to clear the streets of Canisy of rubble caused by Allied bombing. The engineers, like the armored infantry, would soon discard their new camouflage uniforms for fear of friendly fire. *U.S. Army via Real War Photos*

Below: Tanks of the 67th Armored Regiment take up positions near Mortain on August 6, 1944. The German counteroffensive to sever the U.S. front in Normandy would begin at midnight that night. *U.S. Army via Real War Photos*

Brooks received permission to launch his entire CCA in support of the paratroopers.

On June 13 the German attack came in against the airborne troops, whose ranks had been severely depleted since D-Day. Though the paratroopers were the toughest individual fighters in the Allied order of battle, they were stretched thin and had little means of fending off German armor. By mid-afternoon the German onslaught was about to break through, when the defenders suddenly heard gunfire in their rear. The "Hell on Wheels" had arrived just in time. The tankers waded head-on into the German attack, gunning down enemy infantry stretched in two columns on both sides of the road. The Shermans spit cannon fire while commanders manned .50-cal. machine-guns up top and hull machine-gunners swept the field. The Germans had evidently not expected a U.S. armored division to be already ashore and so far inland. Their attack collapsed, while the bone-tired "Screaming Eagles" welcomed their reinforcements.

CCA had lost four tanks and a dozen men in the battle. Afterward up to 800 enemy bodies were counted on the field as opposed to only eight prisoners taken by the "Hell on Wheels". A news article reported that a 2nd Armored officer's only comment was, "Too many prisoners." Later, the division learned that on this day it had earned a new nickname from the German Army: "Roosevelt's Butchers."

After enduring a night of enemy mortar and artillery fire, the 2nd Armored and the 101st Airborne continued driving the 17th SS back the way it had come. On the 13th the remaining gap between the Omaha and Utah beachheads was closed, uniting the entire invasion front into one continuous strip, some 80 miles long but averaging less than 10 miles deep. A CCA task force probing further south toward Périers was pinned down by enemy fire. When the rest of the combat command moved up in support, it too was stopped by anti-tank, mortar and machine-gun fire coming from all sides. It had already become clear that Normandy's terrain would present problems of its own.

Less the 66th Armored's 1st Battalion, which remained to support the 101st Airborne, and later the 83rd Infantry, CCA rejoined CCB in the east. While the defense of Carentan was taking place, the British 7th Armoured Division — the famous "Desert Rats" — had been badly defeated in an attempt to outflank the defenses of Caen at Villers-Bocage. By now the 2nd Panzer Division had appeared on the battlefield and was threatening to attack the weak seam between the American and British beachheads. The 2nd Armored relieved the "Desert Rats" of responsibility for much of the area and supported the British efforts with artillery fire.

In the weeks to come, two different kinds of battles were fought by the Americans and British on the invasion front. Just eight miles from the British beaches was William of Normandy's medieval capital, Caen, beyond which lay flat, open country, including airfields, and a clear route to the Seine and Paris, less than 100 miles away. General Montgomery had planned to capture Caen on D-Day, but the 21st Panzer Division had intervened. On D+1 the 12th SS Panzer (Hitler Youth) arrived, followed by the strongest division in the German Army, Panzer Lehr. 1st SS Panzer, 2nd Panzer, and the 9th and 10th SS Panzer Divisions were dispatched to that sector. On the British side, 7th Armoured was joined by the 11th Armoured, the Guards Armoured Division and later by the Canadian 4th Armoured and several independent tank brigades. Over the next six weeks the vicinity of Caen would see the greatest head-to-head tank battles of the war in the west.

Beyond their beaches on the Cotentin Peninsula, American First Army faced different terrain, of a kind, in fact, that the New World soldiers had never seen. This was hedgerow country, or as the French called it, bocage. Since ancient times, Norman farmers had bordered their fields with rows of trees or bushes, which over the centuries had become veritable walls. A typical hedgerow consisted of a four-foot earthwork packed with roots, topped by dense foliage 12 to 15 feet high. The farmers' fields were irregularly sized and

Above: After running a gauntlet of artillery fire, a 67th Armored Sherman makes it to Calvados, France on August 3, 1944. The beverage named for this town became popular with U.S. troops in Normandy. *U.S. Army via Real War Photos*

shaped, surrounded on all sides by these natural fortifications. Most roads in the area were sunken tracks that passed between adjoining hedgerows, almost like tunnels in the full foliage of summer.

This was terrain in which armor could not be advantageously employed, either for attack or defense. A tank would have both extremely limited mobility and poor fields of fire. Instead, the champion of the hedgerow was the hidden infantryman, overlooking the roads within arms' length of probing vehicles. The Germans had introduced an improved version of their Panzerfaust hand-held anti-tank weapon that summer, capable of destroying armor at 60 yards instead of the previous 30. There was little need for Panzers or even 88mm guns to defend the hedgerow country, when individual infantrymen armed with Panzerfausts, mines, satchel charges and machine guns could defend the claustrophobic roads just as efficiently. To complicate the problem, the area was dotted with marshes and the Germans had flooded still more to confine movement through the countryside. While the British matched armor against armor to reach the open ground beyond Caen, the Americans relied upon their infantry to uproot the concealed enemy among the infernal bocage.

On June 19, the 2nd Armored was pulled into reserve, where it continued to train, and waited for the rest of its units to come across the Channel, a process that would be completed on July 2. On the 20th, two Luftwaffe aircraft bombed the bivouac of the 67th Armored's 2nd Battalion, inflicting a huge crater and 58 casualties. At that time, too, a gigantic storm swept the Normandy coast, wrecking the Allies' artificial harbors (Mulberries), setting back the Allied supply schedule to the tune of 140,000 tons.

Meanwhile, 2nd Armored tankers discussed the hedgerow problem which so far had proven their biggest obstacle. At Carentan, 17th Armored Engineer "tankdozers" — tanks equipped with bulldozer prows — had provided a slow answer. Other tanks that simply tried to drive over the hedges had been anticipated by Germans waiting to fire at their exposed underbellies. Then a sergeant named Curtis Culin devised a solution. Acting upon a suggestion by a man named Roberts, he fixed steel prongs to the front of a tank so that a hedgerow could be sharply uprooted. In a demonstration before American brass, his invention proved efficient and hundreds of U.S. tanks were transformed into "Rhinos," employing the steel girders of Rommel's anti-invasion obstacles.

Another enhancement to the Sherman arrived in the form of a higher-velocity 76mm gun to replace the 75mm. However, the new weapon was undercharged and still too weak to penetrate the frontal armor of a Panther or Tiger. After receiving a report from Bradley, a bitter Eisenhower said: "Ordnance told me this 76 would take care of anything the Germans had. Now I find you can't knock out a damn thing with it." It was as if, in mid-1944, the U.S. had upgunned the Sherman to the same degree the Germans had upgunned their Mark IV two years earlier. But this still left the Panthers and Tigers as kings of the jungle.

After the unification of the U.S. beachheads, Bradley focused northwest toward the tip of the Cotentin Peninsula, where lay the deep-water port of Cherbourg. Its capture was considered integral to Overlord for solving the supply problem, and in the meantime other U.S. offensive action was prohibited save for steady pressure on the ground and further attrition of the enemy through air attacks. J. Lawton ("Lightning Joe") Collins' VII Corps was given the task of subduing the northern Cotentin, against weak infantry opposition that mainly retreated into Cherbourg's fortress defenses. Among prisoners taken were hundreds of Russian or Polish men who had been conscripted into the Wehrmacht.

Cherbourg fell on June 27 but by then the Germans had so thoroughly demolished its port facilities that it did not become fully operational until September. On June 30, 2nd Armored, now part of Charles Corlett's XIX Corps, moved to positions southwest of Bayeux to support the British flank. Keeping its tanks in reserve, 2AD recon and armored infantry skirmished with the Germans and its armored artillery dueled with German guns. It was during this period that the 2nd Armored first made contact with its enemy counterpart, the 2nd Panzer Division. These two elite formations would come to know each other well as the war progressed.

On July 3 Bradley launched a general offensive across his front, designed to drive through the hedgerow country to reach the open spaces beyond. But this infantry offensive was hampered by rain — which not only kept Allied aircraft out of the battle but allowed the Germans to direct their firepower against predictable approach routes between the flooded areas. After a week of incurring 30,000 casualties with little gain, Bradley called off the offensive. On July 7 Montgomery launched his own infantry in Operation Charnwood, which succeeded in capturing half of Caen up to the Orne River. By then Caen had been bombed into rubble and vehicles could not pass through the streets. German infantry clung to the southern half of town while the 12th SS Panzer waited defiantly on the outskirts for Montgomery's next attempt.

After a full month of largely static attritional battle, the spectre of the Great War stalemate in the West had begun to raise its ugly head. Both army commanders, Montgomery and Bradley, turned to the Allied strategic air forces for a means to break the deadlock. Since D-day, the four-engine heavies of the Eighth Air Force and British Bomber Command had been overflying the battle to bomb the German homeland. It was now requested that they assist the Allied armies on the continent in a tactical role. Eisenhower facilitated the idea against the protests of the bomber chiefs, most of whom thought that strategic air power could win the war by itself. The airmen only reluctantly agreed to aid the armies.

On July 18, Montgomery launched Operation Goodwood. Some 2,000 Allied heavy bombers laid an explosive carpet south of Caen and then the ground attack kicked off with three armored divisions in the center, infantry divisions advancing on the shoulders. The Germans were stunned by the carpet bombing, but as the smoke cleared they managed to assemble a defense. The key positions south of Caen were held by the I SS Panzer Corps, supported by the 21st Panzer Division and elements of the 2nd. The II SS Panzer Corps, consisting of the 9th and 10th SS Panzer Divisions, counterattacked the British right at the same time as the weather closed in, stripping away Allied air support. After three days, and the loss of some 400 tanks and 5,500 men, Montgomery concluded his offensive.

General Bradley, too, had devised an attack employing Allied strategic air power to pave the way, but the same rains that concluded the Goodwood operation stalled his own offensive. Bradley planned to lay his own bombing carpet on a very narrow sector — only some 6,000 yards wide and 2,500 yards deep — just to the southwest of the town of St. Lô. In the preceding week he had expended roughly 5,000 infantry casualties to gain St. Lô and its highway, an old Roman road, that stretched straight west to Périers. It was a clear demarcation between U.S. lines and German. The sector south of the road was now held by the Panzer Lehr Division, supported by two German paratrooper regiments. The 2nd Armored moved west for the operation and was temporarily attached to VII Corps.

Above: Armored cars of the 82nd Reconnaissance Battalion wind through the streets of Calvados in Normandy on August 3, 1944. On its way to the town the 82nd had run into a bloody ambush in the forest of St. Sever. In picture are two M8 Greyhounds — wheeled armored cars that had a turret-mounted .50-cal MG and a crew of three.
U.S. Army via Real War Photos

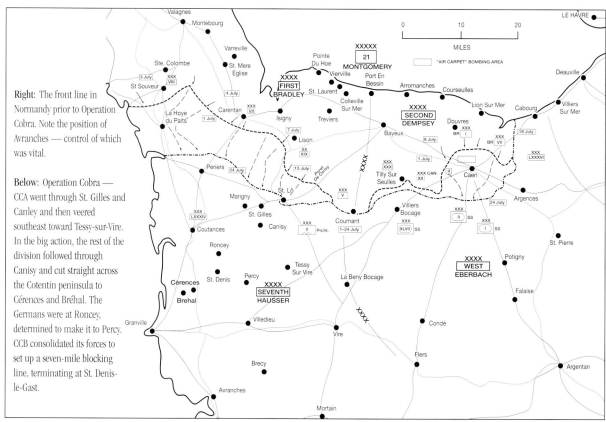

Right: The front line in Normandy prior to Operation Cobra. Note the position of Avranches — control of which was vital.

Below: Operation Cobra — CCA went through St. Gilles and Canley and then veered southeast toward Tessy-sur-Vire. In the big action, the rest of the division followed through Canisy and cut straight across the Cotentin peninsula to Cérences and Bréhal. The Germans were at Roncey, determined to make it to Percy. CCB consolidated its forces to set up a seven-mile blocking line, terminating at St. Denis-le-Gast.

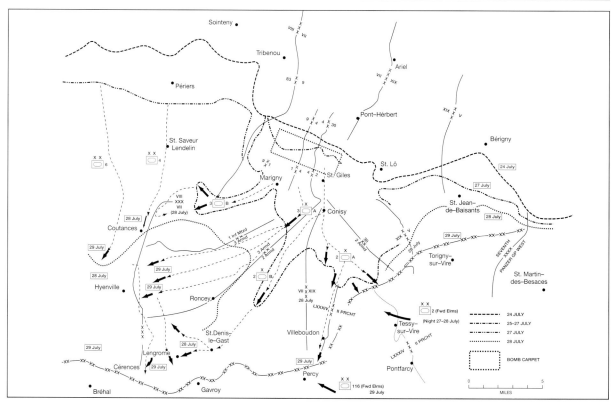

On July 12–13, advance elements of 2nd Armored Division encountered a new enemy *Doppelgänger*, the 2nd SS Panzer Division (*Das Reich*), which had deployed units to stiffen the German left.

Collins' VII Corps would initiate the offensive with its 30th, 4th and 9th Infantry Divisions lined up abreast, and the 2nd and 3rd Armored Divisions and (motorized) 1st Infantry Division held in reserve to exploit any breakthroughs. Troy Middleton's VIII Corps on the American right would join the offensive a day later. The idea was that VII Corps would uproot the Germans from their line at St. Lô and then VIII Corps would sweep in to crush the retreating Germans against the VII Corps' anvil. It was thought that several German divisions could be trapped north of a line stretching to Coutances on the Cotentin coast. Ultimately, the key city for both sides was Avranches, which sat at the southwestern end of the peninsula. As long as the Germans held Avranches, U.S. First Army would remain cooped up in the Cotentin. But if the Americans gained it they would have a gateway into the remainder of France.

Allied strength in France was now approaching 1,500,000 men, and they had more tanks, armored vehicles and ammunition crammed into the invasion area than they could profitably use. George Patton had arrived on the continent, anxiously waiting to activate his U.S. Third Army to exploit any breakthrough. But the breakthrough would first have to be accomplished by First Army, in which Patton's only divisional command, the 2nd Armored, would play the primary role.

Above: American units advance near Coutances. The buildings on the other side give testimony to the ferocity of the bombardment which proceeded them. By the time Coutances was captured by U.S. troops, on July 28, 1944, it had been all but abandoned by the Germans. *U.S. Army via Real War Photos*

Below: Roscoe Lewis of the division's 48th Armored Medical Battalion relaxes with a copy of *Life* magazine in Normandy in summer 1944. *Courtesy of Mark Bando*

OPERATION COBRA

The U.S. offensive got off to a false start on July 24 when thousands of aircraft lifted off from England, only to find a cloud-shrouded target area. The attack was immediately called off, though some bomb groups didn't get the word. They not only delivered ordnance on the Germans but on the U.S. 30th Infantry Division, which suffered 156 casualties.

The next morning Eighth Air Force heavies came in again, this time accidentally inflicting 601 casualties on the 30th, 9th and 4th Infantry Divisions and killing Lt. General Lesley McNair, the highest ranking American to die in the war. But demoralizing as these short bombs were to the U.S. infantry on their start-lines, the Panzer Lehr Division suffered far more. The attacks began with hundreds of fighter-bombers knocking out AA sites and dropping napalm. Then over 1,500 heavies dropped 4,400 tons of explosives on the narrow sector, followed by 350 medium bombers pulverizing anything that might still be moving. All this time, 1,000 U.S. artillery pieces fired into the maelstrom. Fritz Bayerlein, the commander of Panzer Lehr, responded to exhortations from his high command to hold the line in almost plaintive terms. All his forward units were still in place, he said, "Because they are dead."

Incredibly, when the U.S. infantry began to advance around 1:00 on July 25, they immediately met return fire. German artillery blasted the attackers and isolated strongpoints still held out at the front. The offensive made barely a mile on the first day — the infantry had learned through experience to be cautious among the hedgerows. Among U.S. chiefs, pessimism about the utility of carpet bombing set in and Eisenhower, for one, vowed never to bother with such a blunt cudgel again. But VII Corps' Joe Collins had received a number of positive reports during the afternoon. Stalking through the moonscape of craters, his men did not see an overwhelming number of German corpses, but everywhere was evidence of destroyed equipment or abandoned strongpoints. Some units had met no resistance and, despite the usual German practice, they had not received any counterattacks. It occurred to Collins that perhaps the bombing had worked

after all. He decided to throw the dice. Instead of waiting for his infantry to complete the breakthrough he committed his mobile divisions. 2nd Armored would attack on the left (east) of the penetration and 3rd Armored on the right.

Just before 10:00 a.m. on July 26, Maurice Rose's CCA of the 2nd Armored kicked off from its start-line. Riding the tanks of the 66th Armored were 4th Division infantry, their initial objective the village of St. Gilles on the southeast corner of the bomb zone. The 3rd Armored with 1st Infantry troops attacked on the right toward Marigny on the southwest corner.

In St. Gilles, CCA plowed through scattered survivors of Panzer Lehr and debris left by the bombing. On the way to the next town, Canisy, a German tank suddenly turned onto the road and began driving next to the CCA column in the opposite direction. As the Panzer roared by, none of the startled men had time to swing a turret or fire. Finally the German tank reached another corner and, before turning off, its commander popped out of the turret and tossed a grenade into a truck of infantry, causing 19 casualties. After securing Canisy, CCA received orders to veer east, toward Tessy-sur-Vire, in order to hold Cobra's left flank against German reinforcements expected from the east.

That night, Isaac White learned that his CCB would jump off the next morning. The 17th Armored Engineers spent the night ironing out the roads, filling in craters or clearing debris. Attached to CCB were 4th Division infantrymen, the 195th AA Battalion, 702nd Battalion TDs and assorted artillery units, altogether 11,000 men. Preceded by 82nd Recon troops, the command began its attack at 10:00 on July 27.

At first CCB followed CCA's path through St. Gilles and Canisy, but then White received new orders from General Brooks. He was now to veer southwest, taking the shortest route across the peninsula to "cut off withdrawal of enemy from the north." On Cobra's right flank, the 3rd Armored Division had taken Marigny but had been stalled in its drive on Coutances. On the far U.S. right, VIII Corps had stumbled out of the blocks. Middleton's 8th and 90th Divisions had suffered 1,150 casualties the previous day and taken only 100 prisoners. This situation had continued on the 27th when VIII Corps struggled with dense minefields. The Germans had obviously been uprooted from the Cotentin but it was too late to form a blocking line behind the retreating enemy at Coutances. Now it would have to be done by 2nd Armored's CCB, driving for the town of Cérences farther south.

Speed became the priority as CCB columns headed into the German rear regardless of their flanks. German fireblocks of Panzers or anti-tank guns still sprinkled the route but, the farther the 2AD penetrated, the more confused the enemy appeared. A recon platoon of 67th Armored found scores of Germans sleeping in a field. After the Germans were awoken to be made prisoner, a German officer made a break for it, running to a house. The platoon opened up with Tommy guns but the stream of bullets missed. The German then emerged from the house with nine other officers with hands up. An advance patrol of 17th Armored Engineers raced down the roads with German prisoners on the hoods of their jeeps. During the afternoon they shot up an enemy halftrack crew fixing a flat tire. One company of Germans was surprised while lining up for payroll, and both they and the money were captured (one of several troves of currency found during the breakthrough). A ruckus occurred later when a wounded 2AD man was evacuated to England and a doctor asked how he had come to possess so many francs. The Army launched an official investigation.

The 1st Recon Platoon of 67th Armored burst into the town of Nôtre Dame de Cenilly, surprising a number of Germans on the streets. As the Germans ducked for cover, the recon men continued out the other side of town without firing. Then the full 1st Battalion rode in, led by Lt. Colonel Richard Nelson. Germans began running out of a church and Nelson, manning the turret machine gun of his M5, mowed them down on the steps. Two trucks of German infantry pulled up and American fire piled up some 40 bodies. Lt. Col.

Below: A Sherman of Maurice Rose's Combat Command A maneuvers during Operation Cobra, July 26, 1944. *U.S. Army via Chris Ellis*

Nelson was killed the next day. Coming across a burning Stuart on the road south of Nôtre Dame, he approached to investigate, but as he stood in his turret the next round from the German gun took his head off.

Late on the 27th, an 82nd Recon company fought its way into the village of Dangy, destroying a German Panther, five halftracks, some horsedrawn ammunition carts and a command car. What they didn't know was that Dangy was the joint headquarters of the 275th Division and Panzer Lehr, and that General Bayerlein was holding a staff meeting there at the time. While 2nd Armored recon troops battled his headquarters company in the streets, Bayerlein slipped out a back way. This former stalwart of the Afrika Korps and commander of Panzer Lehr, once the most powerful unit in the German Army, was now forlorn. As he hid in the woods he must have repeated to himself one of his last reports to Army Group B: "My division has been annihilated."

By 2:00 a.m. CCB was bedding down for the night, often having to clear their bivouac areas of German stragglers, sometimes fighting off enemy columns unaware that 2AD was in their midst. In the morning, the U.S. tanks and armored infantry probed further along the Norman roads, forging a narrow corridor behind the German front. At times, roving patrols caused more damage to the enemy than they realized. On July 28 a company of the 41st Armored Infantry was advancing on foot. Spotting a German staff car coming down the road, the men laid low on either side and ambushed it, shooting the three occupants. Unknown to the 2AD men, they had killed Lt. Colonel Christian Tychsen, the acting commander of the 2nd SS Panzer Division. The 33-year-old Tychsen, a much decorated hero of the Russian Front, had been returning from a conference with 17th SS commander Otto Baum. Baum now assumed command of both his own division and *Das Reich*.

On the 28th, the 82nd Reconnaissance Battalion once again spearheaded CCB's forward advance, its C Company reaching the Sienne River at midday. This effectively completed 2nd Armored's line across the Cotentin. Along the way the company captured a German field hospital and shot up a number of German trucks, cars and motorcycles that crossed its path. British Typhoon fighter-bombers had flown high-level guard, destroying targets ahead of the company and on its flanks. Crossing the unguarded Sienne to Cérences, the recon men captured a company of German troops at a gasoline dump. One halftrack moved on to the village of Bréhal within sight of the Atlantic Ocean. When it received orders to pull back for the night, C Company had to let its captured German supply troops go, but the 2AD men still had the satisfaction of knowing they had made the deepest penetration of the front by any Allied unit since D-day.

On that same July 28, Middleton's 4th Armored Division rode into Coutances, which by then was undefended. Though Coutances had been intended as the primary objective of Operation Cobra, now a far greater danger to the enemy had appeared in the form of 2nd Armored's dissection of the entire German left.

Corlett's XIX Corps, to the east of VII Corps, was anxious to participate in the battle and 2nd Armored's CCA reverted to that corps, spearheading its drive parallel to the Vire River. Leading the reinforcements Field Marshal Gunther von Kluge was moving from his right to his left was the 2nd Panzer Division, and now 2nd Armored's CCA grappled with it head to head outside Tessy-sur-Vire. Also moving west was the 116th Panzer Division,

Above: Another view of Combat Command A Shermans during Operation Cobra, July 26, 1944.
U.S. Army via Chris Ellis

Above: K. Hanna and Eugene Davidson of the division's 17th Armored Engineer Battalion in Normandy. These men have just discarded their camouflage uniforms and switched back to more standard uniform. *Courtesy of Mark Bando*

formerly the 16th Motorized "Greyhound" Division, made famous during the Stalingrad campaign.

With U.S. VII Corps cutting through their center, VIII Corps pressing against their left, and XIX Corps attempting to cut them off from reinforcement on the right, the Germans in the Cotentin realized that they needed to retreat. The town of Roncey became the assembly point for all forward and rear units dislodged by the offensive. Unfortunately for them, this huge collection of vehicles was perfectly visible from the air, and during the sunny day of July 28 hundreds of British Typhoon and U.S. Thunderbolt fighter-bombers dived on the assemblage. Newly arriving squadrons would circle above, waiting their turn to swoop in. The concentration at Roncey soon became a smoking junkpile of 350 vehicles, though a number of them were merely abandoned as their crews took to the woods.

General Brooks' worry was that 2nd Armored's CCB and CCR, stretched out on a thin line across the peninsula south of Roncey, was now in danger. The German break-out from the Cotentin was likely to come through his command. He pulled his far-flung units back to a seven-mile stretch of road just southeast of Roncey, its terminus at St. Denis-le-Gast. 2nd Armored set up strongpoints at intersections, laying outposts every 200 yards in between, generally positioning its vehicles in fields north of the road. The whole was covered by the divisional artillery, the battalions dispersed at intervals along the line.

The Germans' best option by far was to retreat due south, where a corridor near the coast remained open, and then join their main lines by moving east. But a confusing factor to SS-General Paul Hausser, the commander of Seventh Army, was that the 2nd and 116th Panzer Divisions had been sent to blunt the American offensive in the general direction of the town of Percy, toward the center of the peninsula's base. Instead of ordering his forces to retreat due south to Avranches, he ordered a retreat to the southeast, to connect with the reinforcements at Percy. When von Kluge learned of Hausser's orders he was furious and immediately countermanded them. But by then German communications had been shot. Instead of retreating in such a way as to maintain the vital line across the peninsula to Avranches, the Germans in the Cotentin abandoned the coast. The effect was not only to leave a gap through which the Americans could escape from the Cotentin into the rest of France, it also meant that the Germans would be trying to retreat through the positions of "Hell on Wheels", which now stood smack on a perpendicular line between Roncey and Percy.

Just before dawn on the 29th, a German column led by an 88mm self-propelled gun broke through an intersection held by two CCB companies, one of tanks and one of infantry. The gun plowed all the way through the American position until 2nd Lt. Robert Lotz of the 41st Armored Infantry shot out its periscope with a carbine, then closed in to kill the driver. At daylight the Germans retreated, leaving behind at least 250 dead and some 25 destroyed vehicles. The 88mm SP gun was found with its motor still running and a shell in the breech. The 2AD suffered 29 casualties and the loss of two Shermans and two half-tracks. The 41st took 139 prisoners.

A few hours later, a force of 15 German tanks and 200 paratroopers collided with an outpost company of 4th Infantry protected by four 702nd Battalion Tank Destroyers. After a TD went up in flames, the infantry rushed back into the perimeter of the 78th Armored Field Artillery. Elements of the 82nd Recon and 195th AA Battalion were also in the perimeter. As most of the artillery leveled to fire at the German tanks, the M16 quad .50s of the AA battalion cut bloody swathes through the enemy paratroopers. The Germans veered off, leaving behind seven burning tanks and 126 dead.

During daylight on July 29, the 2AD consolidated its positions. On the night of 29/30 July this seven-mile stretch of road saw the culmination of Operation Cobra. The landscape was alive with *ad hoc* German columns feeling their way southeast, many of them unsure if U.S. tanks and infantry were in their path. Indeed they were. Though deep behind enemy lines, the men of CCB and CCR, 2nd Armored, had manned their stretch of highway against scattered opposition during the daylight hours. After dusk, some dog-tired men went to sleep while others remained at their weapons, suspecting, if not knowing, that they were about to encounter a tidal wave.

That night, all the remaining Germans in the Cotentin were on the move. With his officers all dead or missing, a Panther commander of the 2nd SS Panzer organized a column of 600 men from his own division, the 17th SS, and paratroopers. Heading for

Above: A U.S. column advances west of St. Lô at the start of Operation Cobra, July 25, 1944. Though armor was originally meant to exploit advances made by infantry, the 2nd and 3rd Armored Divisions were released on the second day, when the German front proved to have been shattered by U.S. bombing. *U.S. Army via Chris Ellis*

Above: German units streaming out of the Falaise Gap were pursued across France by Allied fighter-bombers — "Jabos" to their German enemies — and Allied armor. Here German vehicles knocked out by 2nd Armored are left burning on the road to Paris on August 23, 1944. *U.S. Army via Chris Ellis*

Percy in daylight he was attacked from the air during the afternoon and then ran into a 2nd Armored roadblock. To engage in daylight would only invite more wrath from the fighter-bombers, so he veered away. Once darkness had fallen he began his breakout in earnest.

Around midnight the SS column came to an outpost held by the 41st Armored Infantry's 2nd Battalion. Two Shermans overlooked the intersection to the right, with four half-tracks parked in a field just beyond. The Panther leading the German column rolled through the intersection and its commander saw the Shermans, too late to swing his turret. He radioed back for two Sturmgeschütz SP guns behind him to wheel right at the corner and knock them out. Sgt. Ed Fogarty was atop one of the Shermans at the time, trying to warn its commander what was coming down the road. Suddenly the tank's turret was blasted by a 75mm round and Fogarty was thrown 30 feet away. The other Sherman brewed up a few seconds later.

The lead Panther in the column came upon the four 2AD halftracks and calmly traversed its gun sideways to knock them all out. One had been filled with flares and created a huge fireworks display. After blasting its way through the roadblock this column rejoined German lines at Percy.

Another force of Panzers and SP guns accompanied by paratroopers and other mixed units came up against a crossroads held by the headquarters of 67th Armored's 3rd Battalion. On making contact, the Germans began firing to both sides of the road, some men carrying Panzerfausts at the hip, lobbing rounds before them. The Americans were startled but attempted to return fire into the road. One sergeant lay next to a hole in the hedgerow and killed three Germans who tried to crawl through, cutting their throats with a knife. Then a German tank poked its gun through a part of the hedgerow that had concealed 3rd Battalion's headquarters vehicles. The Panzer began methodically destroying the lot, including a Sherman, two SPs, seven halftracks, five trucks, two jeeps, and a towed artillery piece. For good measure, a 41st Armored Infantry ammo truck went up, spraying shrapnel and pyrotechnics over the area.

Retreating men from these two clashes came pouring into 41st Armored Infantry's headquarters area, which itself was under attack. In the black of night it was a challenge for U.S. troops on the move to avoid friendly fire. After a report from Graves Registration the next morning, the Headquarters Company was lauded in an odd Presidential Unit Citation, which said it had: "killed 139 enemy troops on the edge of the defense sector by shots in the head or upper chest, without death or injury to any friendly troops within the same area from friendly fire." It may be a coincidence that 139 is the exact number of prisoners taken by the 41st Armored Infantry the day before. "This magnificent defense," the citation continued, "contributed materially to the sealing off of large numbers of enemy troops in the Cherbourg Peninsula in a major entrapment operation executed by Combat Command B."

At St. Denis-le-Gast, the left terminus of 2AD's line, a platoon of 3rd Battalion tanks was dispatched after nightfall to see what was going on. They found the town full of German armor and infantry heading south. U.S. troops had been forced out of the town. The tank platoon would have been destroyed before it could retreat except that Sgt. Douglas Tanner ran his M5 Stuart forward to face a German 88mm SP gun. In this unequal contest Tanner was killed, but his heroism provided time for the rest of his platoon to withdraw.

Outside St. Denis, American units took cover as German armor and troops poured south. A scout from 67th Armored's Recon Company, Kal Isaacs, recalled: "It was a night of massive, deafening fire, machine-gun tracers, explosions, flares and confusion. I was separated from my platoon and encountered several enemy soldiers and almost blundered into an enemy tank column. In the morning, the fields and forests were littered with bodies, both American and German."

One column of 11 German vehicles made a wrong turn above St. Denis and, since it was going in the wrong direction, drove through several 2AD units unmolested. Finally it entered the positions of the 78th Armored Artillery and an American asked the lead vehicle to identify itself. A surprised German answered, "Was ist das?" Then everyone opened fire. All the German vehicles were destroyed and the next morning the Americans counted 90 dead. The 2AD suffered four dead and seven wounded.

Throughout the hours of darkness, skirmishes and outright battles flared all along 2nd Armored's seven-mile defense line. Creeping German infantry infiltrated the lines while armored columns tried to blast their way through the roadblocks. 2AD's artillery battalions provided fire support or, if under attack themselves, fired away in all directions.

The climax of the chaos came near the hamlet of Grimesnil. The largest German column encountered by CCB that night consisted of some 90 vehicles and 2,500 troops, stretched out in march formation for half a mile. This was a mixed bag of Wehrmacht units, led by a 150mm SP gun, followed by a Sturmgeschütz, and then trucks, halftracks, ambulances and Volkswagens. It first made contact at an

Below: The French "bocage" country combined all the defensive features most likely to cause difficulties for armored units — sunken lanes, deep medieval hedgerows that afforded cover for ambushers, and tree-cover that hid vehicles and troops from Allied aircraft. These British Shermans are seen in the hedgerows during Operation Goodwood, the attack southeast of Caen that ended a week before Operation Cobra. *Via George Forty*

Above: On September 2, 1944, troops of the 41st
Armored Infantry Regiment pass from France into
Belgium during the great pursuit of the German Army
from Normandy. *U.S. Army via Real War Photos*

outpost held by two U.S. halftracks and three Shermans. An American jeep was in the middle of the road. Suddenly the jeep was blasted apart by a 150mm hit, and in the next minute the U.S. halftracks went up in flames. The Shermans retreated slowly down the road in reverse, firing away as they fell back on the stronger 2AD position behind them. This was held by a company of Shermans, a platoon of Stuarts, a company of armored infantry, some armored engineers, and the 2nd Battalion's headquarters group. The call went out for support from the 78th and 62nd Artillery Battalions.

As the German column plunged into the position, the 2AD opened fire. The menacing 150mm SP fell to blasts from a waiting Sherman. A Sturmgeschütz behind it passed the destroyed behemoth but it, too, fell to a 75mm shot through the fighting compartment. Now the German column was stalled in the road as fire came in from both sides. At the rear, 2AD engineers snuck around to knock out a tank, pinning the huge enemy column in place. The Americans poured tank fire, machine-gun fire, and white phosphorous mortar rounds into the column. Men heard female screams because the Germans had tried to bring out some nurses or communications workers. Finally, at about 3:00 a.m., the 2AD artillery opened up, lacing a path of devastation down the narrow strip. The trapped column absorbed 700 shells. A number of Germans took to the fields on either side of the road — two 2AD men who had gone to sleep nearby were later found dead — but on the road itself, confused fighting lasted nearly until dawn. During this action, Horel B. Whittington earned the 2nd Armored's first Congressional Medal of Honor. (See page 87.)

It was not until 9:00 in the morning on July 30 that 2AD men moved in to investigate the carnage. Major Jerome Smith called it: "The most Godless sight I have ever witnessed on any battlefield." Amid the wreckage of all 90 vehicles of the German column were some 450 dead, a precise number difficult to determine because body parts were all over the landscape; clumps of others were welded by fire to the surfaces of their vehicles. The first task was to clear the road with bulldozers. Hundreds of prisoners were also taken. The 2nd Armored defenders lost fewer than 50 men.

On July 30, elements of the 4th Armored Division, rushing down from VIII Corps, entered Avranches on the Atlantic coast. The town had been all but abandoned, its bridges intact, even though it was integral to preventing a U.S. breakout into France. Hausser's decision to aim his retreating units southeast, toward Percy, was now seen to be one of the worst German decisions of the campaign. And it was even worse for the Germans who had tried to break through the U.S. armored cordon. 2nd Armored's CCB had suffered some 400 casualties during Operation Cobra, but they had killed at least 1,500 Germans and captured 5,200 more.

THE BREAK-OUT

Patton's Third Army was activated on August 1, and he immediately funneled six divisions through the gap at Avranches into the open plains of France. The entire German position in Normandy had been compromised, U.S. troops now flowing behind their front. Fortunately for the Germans, a pre-conceived Allied notion was that the Brittany peninsula, which pointed into the Atlantic south of the Cotentin, was essential to their strategy. Thus Patton dispatched two full corps into a cul de sac to the west, while the Germans' true peril lay in U.S. advances to the east. In addition, Patton aimed his remaining corps to the southeast, where it seized Le Mans, Orleans and other towns, the men joyriding through throngs of jubilant French civilians. These spectacular advances prompted huge headlines in the States, though they were not strongly opposed by the enemy.

Back at the front, 2nd Armored's CCA was now grappling with the 2nd and 116th Panzer Divisions along the River Vire. While CCB and CCR had been standing against the German breakout from the Cotentin, CCA had been exchanging head-to-head blows with the German reinforcements arriving from the east. By the time Tessy fell on August 2, 66th Armored's 3rd Battalion had lost over 100 percent of its tanks, three-quarters of its officers and nearly half of its enlisted men. That same day, a company of the 82nd Recon Battalion hastily made its way through the dense forest of St. Sever toward the town of Calvados. Coming to a roadblock of felled trees, the column had halted to investigate when two hidden Tigers opened fire. German infantry concealed in the foliage poured machine-gun and mortar fire up and down the column. The Americans scrambled back, leaving behind 25 dead. CCA's main strength switched to the large town of Vire, which was tenaciously held by the Germans. On August 5, Brig. General Maurice Rose of CCA was promoted to command the 3rd Armored Division. Colonel John Collier, leader of the 66th Armored, took over CCA.

As Patton's Third Army spilled in all directions behind the German front in Normandy, Adolf Hitler' situation maps in East Prussia appeared to reveal an opportunity. Third Army's break-out had only taken place through a tiny corridor along the coast at Avranches. The Americans had poured three full corps through this corridor, but just a brief, violent counterattack through Mortain could close it. Third Army would be left out on a vine and First Army could be routed on its flank. To this point the U.S. Army had not been subjected to a full-blooded, multi-divisional Panzer attack since Kasserine. And in Hitler's mind there was every possibility it would once again collapse.

Through Ultra intercepts, Bradley learned of the German plan with just hours to spare. The 2nd Armored had fully reverted to XIX Corps on August 2, but now its CCB was again lent to Collins' VII Corps. It moved toward Barenton on the southern flank of the impending offensive. CCA remained around Vire supporting the 28th and 29th Infantry Divisions on the northern flank. In front of the German thrust was the 30th Infantry, flanked by regiments of the 4th and 9th Infantry Divisions, supported by the 3rd Armored. The 30th had just moved into the foxholes of the 1st Infantry that evening, the "Big Red One" withdrawing into Corps reserve. The 35th Infantry Division was put at VII Corps' disposal, backed up by two more divisions of Patton's army should they be required.

At midnight on August 6/7, the German counteroffensive got underway. Without artillery preparation, the Panzers roared through the night, overrunning Mortain and several advanced infantry companies. The 30th Infantry Division took the brunt of the offensive, proceeding to write a record of unparalleled heroism in U.S. history. On the flanks, the Germans ran into a wall of steel; even worse for them, the 7th dawned clear and Allied fighter-bombers began swarming the skies overhead. American fighters headed inland to hold off the Luftwaffe, while British fighter-bombers attacked the Panzers. German soldiers dubbed August 7 the "Day of the Typhoon."

After First Army had confidently stopped the enemy's forward momentum, the battle devolved into a static slugging match. The Germans had gotten to within nine miles of Avranches but could advance no further. The 2nd Armored, facing elements of the 2nd Panzer, 2nd SS Panzer and Panzer Lehr around Barenton, and the 116th Panzer and 3rd Parachute Division around Vire, exchanged heavy blows with the rim of the German salient. On August 11 von Kluge, who had not wanted to launch the offensive in the first place, persuaded Hitler to allow a withdrawal. The British had opened up a new offensive to the northeast

Below: U.S. units pass German Panzer IVs abandoned or knocked out during the advance.
U.S. Army via Chris Ellis

Right: An M4 speeds past a knocked out German 88mm on August 15, 1944. The "88" started life as an anti-aircraft gun but turned into the most effective anti-tank gun of the war. The 88 was often deployed — as in this case — on its carriage to allow speedy repositioning to avoid counter-battery fire. Note the Culin hedgerow device on the front of the M4. Many of these "Rhino" tanks were created — using Rommel's former beach obstacles — to cut openings through the hedgerows in Normandy. *U.S. Army via George Forty*

Below right: During the breakout across France, 2nd Armored enjoyed the benefit of intelligence from friendly civilians. Here a Frenchman points out German positions to men of the 41st Armored Infantry on August 21, 1944. *U.S. Army via Real War Photos*

2ND ARMORED ORGANIC UNITS
(units that served through the war)

Headquarters Company
Service Company
Combat Command A
Combat Command B
41st Armored Infantry Regiment
66th Armored Regiment
67th Armored Regiment
17th Armored Engineer Battalion
82nd Armored Reconnaissance
  Battalion
142nd Armored Signal Company
2nd Armored Division Artillery
14th Armored Field Artillery Battalion
78th Armored Field Artillery Battalion
92nd Armored Field Artillery Battalion
2nd Armored Division Trains
2nd Ordnance Maintenance Battalion
Supply Battalion
48th Armored Medical Battalion
Military Police Platoon

Near-constant attachments in the ETO:
702nd Tank Destroyer Battalion
195th Anti-Aircraft Battalion

that threatened to crush the entire German position in Normandy. On that front only the ruthless Hitler Youth of the 12th SS Panzer Division remained like a jagged rock to stem a flow of British armor.

The counteroffensive at Mortain had thrust the Germans' main strength deeper to the west, exactly when U.S. strength was flowing behind them to the east. The opportunity for a great encirclement battle now existed, should the Allied high command realize it. Toward this end, Bradley ordered Patton's XV Corps to halt its advance into the empty interior of France and head due north, to Argentan. At the same time, Montgomery launched his Canadian Army toward Falaise, thence 12 miles more to Argentan, to trap all German forces in Normandy in a pocket. In the next few days, Hitler caved in to his generals' urgent requests to pull back the Normandy front. Key to his decision was Field Marshal Walther Model's assuming command in Normandy, replacing von Kluge, who had replaced Rommel. The Führer's trust in Model — his "fireman" who had retrieved several previous crises in Russia — remained firm, and when Model assessed that the situation called for withdrawal, Hitler had to take heed.

Once the Germans began to retreat from Mortain, 2nd Armored found easier going with its relentless attacks on enemy-held hills, villages and forests. But the countryside still swarmed with German rearguards and isolated units. On August 13, a popular officer of the 82nd Recon, Lt. Morris Eustis, was killed in an ambush. While leaning out the turret of his Sherman talking to some men, a Panzerfaust round from a hedgerow blew him and his tank to pieces. Afterward, four Germans in the bushes surrendered and it was said that one of them bragged about "killing your lieutenant." The POW cages were a 30-minute walk to the rear, but the private who escorted the prisoners was told to be back in 10 minutes. Four shots were heard from an M1 carbine and the private returned. On August 15 the 2nd Armored was pulled into reserve for rest and maintenance, while the division as a whole reverted once more to XIX Corps.

The remainder of the Normandy campaign can be described as a disastrous German defeat, with the important proviso that with the ratios of strength and positional advantage then so heavily in favor of the Allies, the Wehrmacht in the West could have been utterly ruined. Once Patton's XV Corps had arrived at Argentan, Bradley refused to allow it to proceed to Falaise, a move that would have closed the pocket. Among his several, almost equally absurd, rationales, was the fear that U.S. and Canadian forces would accidentally fire on each other if they completed the encirclement. The main strength of Haislip's XV Corps, bored with standing at Argentan, moved on toward the Seine, and when Bradley finally recognized that the Falaise Gap needed to be closed, the effort was clumsy and delayed. A 12-mile escape gap was left open to the Germans until August 22.

The great drama of the Falaise pocket resulted in 10,000 German dead and 50,000 captured, from the last 90–100,000 men evacuated from Normandy. But prior to that final Götterdämmerung, a total of some 300,000 German troops and 25,000 vehicles had escaped across the Seine. In the years since, the Allied victory has often been exaggerated by citing figures from the last German combat troops to make it out of the inferno. The 1st SS Panzer Division, for example, is often said to have emerged from Normandy with only 300 survivors. In fact, though the division lost about 5,000 men during the campaign (and nearly all of its front-line equipment), the division's authorized complement was 22,000. In September 1944, the German armaments industry would reach a new peak in production. In the months to come the "Hell on Wheels", like other U.S. divisions, would find their old antagonists, including the 2nd Panzer, 9th Panzer, Panzer Lehr and SS *Das Reich* — all supposedly destroyed in Normandy — back at full strength and re-equipped. The failure of the Allies to go for the jugular in Normandy would soon come back to haunt them.

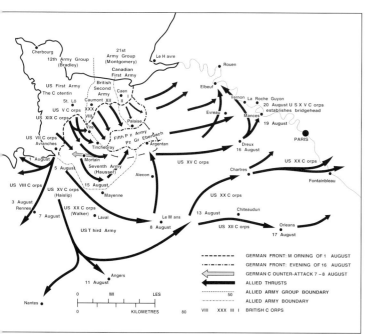

As it stood, the U.S. 12th and British 21st Army Groups enjoyed an exhilarating ride across 300 to 400 miles of French and Belgian territory during the late summer of 1944, chasing a vanquished enemy before them. Until the Germans finally arrived at another line that they meant to hold.

IN PURSUIT

On August 18, 1944, the 2nd Armored began moving east, passing south of the ongoing conflagration in the Falaise Pocket. At one point they had to wait at an intersection to allow the jubilant 2nd French Armored Division to pass through on its way to liberate Paris. On the 20th the 2AD attacked north to the Seine River with the 30th Infantry Division on its right and the 28th Infantry on its left. The idea was that any Germans not trapped at Falaise could still be cut off at the Seine.

Initial opposition was light, but blown bridges and streams prevented fast progress. Advancing north on parallel roads, the division scooped up hundreds of

Above: The breakout from Normandy and advance to the Seine. The Allies had a chance to trap the Fifth Panzer Army in the Falaise Pocket, but in spite of severe attrition many German units were able to escape.

German stragglers, as well as bottles of champagne and cognac, and fruit and flowers from cheering French civilians. At the Avre River, CCB ran into a tough enemy force that was trying to hold open a crossing point for retreating troops at Verneuil. Artillery and anti-tank fire caused heavy 2AD casualties on the town's approaches and at one point Captain John Erbes of the 48th Armored Medical Battalion had to wave a Red Cross flag. The Germans held their fire while his medics evacuated the wounded. Erbes eventually became the most decorated medical officer of the war.

Ordered to bypass the strongpoint, CCB crossed the Avre several miles upriver. On the open roads, both CCA and CCB encountered ragged German formations of all sizes, blowing them away, capturing them, or forcing them to scatter in woods. The 82nd Recon, as ever in the lead, surprised a column of retreating troops and destroyed 14 vehicles, taking 274 prisoners. By now the 2AD was closing in on its objective, the town of Elbeuf, a major German crossing point on the Seine.

Sweeping west of Elbeuf to cut its access roads, the 67th Armored's 3rd Battalion lost three tanks to a German ambush. The battalion recoiled and then surged forward under artillery fire, flushing out two Panthers, which were quickly destroyed. In Elbeuf, the 116th Panzer Division had been ordered to make a stand until other units got across the Seine. The Germans considered this bridgehead so important that even the Luftwaffe made an appearance to stave off the "Hell on Wheels". On the 26th, CCA attacked from the south and got into the outskirts of town, but by nightfall the men had been pinned down by intense fire. Meanwhile, the 41st Armored Infantry had captured a German courier who said that 116th Panzer was preparing to withdraw at midnight. CCA attacked again at dawn and mopped up the center of town against last-ditch holdouts.

During the afternoon General Brooks was informed that Elbeuf was outside First Army's sector and had to be handed over to the British. When the Canadian 7th Brigade rolled in, CCA commander John Collier and Sidney Hinds of the 41st Armored Infantry requested a receipt for the town so that the British couldn't claim its capture. On the way back from this meeting, Hinds was caught in a Nebelwerfer barrage fired from across the river. After medics had plucked the shrapnel chunks from his arm he refused to be evacuated.

The 2nd Armored was ordered to move 45 miles southeast, where after two days of rest it joined Haislip's XV Corps to cross the Seine on August 29. On the far side of the river the 2AD returned to Corlett's XIX Corps, which also included the 30th and 79th Infantry Divisions. The question now became whether the Germans could retreat faster than the Americans could pursue. Though enemy Panzer and a few select Panzergrenadier divisions were fully motorized, the bulk of the German Army was horsedrawn, its artillery and supply vehicles easy prey for the Allied fighter-bombers that raked the roads ahead of the advance. And German horses (along with French cattle) had been prominent among the victims of airpower in Normandy. When a column was caught by fighter-bombers, men could run off to either side to take cover but the horses would remain sitting ducks in harness. By this time most of the German Army was on foot, save cars or trucks they could seize from civilians.

On August 30, XIX Corps kicked off with 2nd Armored in the center, making excellent progress through a scattering of firefights. After dark, a company of 82nd Recon was driving up a road when the rear vehicle radioed the commander that a German column was charging up behind them as if they wanted to pass. The Recon men stopped and pulled to the side, and when the German column came abreast they blasted it off the road.

Relations between the British and American high commands had been difficult ever since North Africa, and now 2nd Armored became a pawn in the struggle. General Montgomery, the commander of British 21st Army Group, had secured permission to use the Allied airborne forces in a drop on the Belgian city of Tournai. Omar Bradley, commanding the American 12th Army Group, protested vehemently, maintaining that airlift capacity should be devoted to delivering gasoline and ammunition to the advancing ground forces. He further claimed that his First Army spearheads could take Tournai before the paratroopers — scheduled to drop on September 3 — could get there.

On the night of August 31, 2nd Armored's General Brooks was visited by XIX Corps staff officers who informed him of an "impossible" assignment. On orders from General Bradley he was to seize the city of Tournai by midnight on September 2. "Get a good night's sleep," Brooks assured the officers. "It's in the bag." Then he unfolded some maps with his own chief of staff, Colonel Charles Palmer, to find where Tournai was. It was across the Belgian border in front of the British zone.

At daybreak on September 1, 2nd Armored headed north in its customary formation, CCA on the right, CCB on the left, and CCR behind in the center. 82nd Recon's Company A subsequently became the first Allied unit into Belgium. German resistance was not as troublesome as the hordes of Belgian civilians throwing fruit and beverages. One 41st Regiment officer was knocked out by a beer bottle thrown at his head. The next day, General Brooks and the commander of CCR, Colonel Hinds, were talking at an intersection while waiting for CCA to drive by. After it had gone, a Frenchman came tearing up on a bicycle, pointing behind him, shouting "Les Boches, les Boches!" Brooks asked, "How many?' and as the Frenchman sped by he yelled, "Beaucoup, beaucoup!" Just then, a huge German column came churning down the road. Brooks and Hinds grabbed machine guns but the one on Brooks' halftrack jammed. They took off across the field while radioing for help. Tanks and halftracks from CCA circled back and surrounded the German column. Thirty prisoners were taken, next to 300 enemy dead and 123 destroyed vehicles.

At 10:00 p.m. on September 2, elements of CCA seized Tournai, two hours ahead of the midnight schedule. Bradley was vindicated and Montgomery's airborne operation was called off. Nevertheless, the operation roused ire in the British Guards Armoured Division. Its commander sent Brooks a note expressing "hope that 2AD understands Tournai to be totally within the British Zone." But by now the 2nd Armored couldn't leave. It was out of fuel. Because the Allied transport force had been tied up for five days for

Below: 1st Sergeant Edward B. Menker of Company B, 41st Armored Infantry. *Courtesy of Mark Bando*

Above: Charles Rost of the 67th Armored Regiment posing with his 2nd Armored shoulder patch on prominent display. *Courtesy of Mark Bando*

Above right: Infantry push ahead under supporting fire from tanks, September 1944. *U.S. Army via Chris Ellis*

Below right: Major Harry H. Hart of the 14th Armored Field Artillery Battalion. Note on his cap the distinctive pin of the 14th AFA. *Courtesy of Mark Bando*

the cancelled paratrooper operation, the front had had been deprived of 5,000 tons of supplies.

The 2nd Armored remained around Tournai for three days. When the first gasoline stocks arrived they went to the 79th Infantry Division so it could move south to join Patton's Third Army. By the time XIX Corps — now consisting of only 2AD and the 30th Infantry — was fully refueled, Collins' VII Corps and Gerow's V Corps to its right had jumped ahead, already across the Meuse River.

On September 5, 2AD kicked off again, toward the Albert Canal, which bisected Belgium inland from Antwerp. 82nd Recon led the way, taking bags of prisoners en route. These were not always German combat troops but Luftwaffe flak units, occupation troops or other rear units disoriented or stranded in the general retreat. In an ominous development for the Allies, German Fifteenth Army, withdrawing from Calais, was then taking up positions in the Schelde Estuary north of Antwerp. Montgomery had seized the great port of Antwerp on the 4th, but hadn't considered that the facilities would be useless as long as the Germans held the approaches.

Meanwhile, due to the excellent performance of 2nd Armored in the campaign, Edward Brooks was promoted to corps command. His replacement was none other than "Old Gravel Voice," Ernest Harmon, who had led the 2AD in North Africa. After 1st Armored's debacle at Kasserine, Harmon had taken over that division and led it in the Italian campaign, including the breakout from Anzio to seize Rome. He had been promoted to command a new XXIII Corps forming up back in the States, but U.S. Chief of Staff George Marshall asked him if he would rather return to the 2nd Armored. At that time, many on the Allied side thought the war was almost finished, the Allied armies already closing up to the German border. Harmon eagerly accepted the offer to forego rank and get in with his old division on what he thought would be the culminating blows of the war.

But his first problem was to cross the Albert Canal. The bridges across this deep body of water had all been blown and the far side was heavily defended. To 2AD's left, the Guards Armoured had already established a crossing at Beringen, and the British gave permission for the 82nd Recon Battalion to cross over that bridge. The 82nd then drove south to clear the far bank in front of 2nd Armored. After making good progress on September 11, the recon troops were counterattacked the next morning and driven back. Two hours later the 82nd attacked again and ran into a roadblock built around a destroyed British armored car. As soon as they tried to bypass this obstacle the 82nd lost five tanks to mines and anti-tank fire. Lt. Colonel Wheeler Merriam rode up to investigate the delay and his halftrack took a hit, seriously wounding his driver and radioman. On September 13, Combat Command A passed over the bridge at Beringen, after which it cleared the opposite banks of the canal. CCB crossed a few days later on a bridge built by Engineers.

The 2nd Armored had now arrived at a thin southern peninsula of Dutch territory bordered by Belgium on one side and Germany on the other. On the west side was the Dutch city of Maastricht and on the east, just across the border, lay Charlemagne's medieval capital, the German city of Aachen. But now the 2AD was meeting resistance on every side; the days of fast pursuit were over. Aside from newly determined German units, a Dutch SS regiment was in the area, fighting with ferocity based on desperation.

On the 16th, Harmon launched a set-piece attack with CCA and CCB lined up abreast on a seven-mile front. After three days, during which 66th Armored fought off a counterattack by German tanks, the division had fought forward less than five miles. At this point the gasoline shortage had been replaced by a shortage of artillery ammunition, and VII Corps to the right was having problems of its own. An attack for the 20th was cancelled and the 2nd Armored took up defensive positions.

In mid-September the entire strategic picture changed from the heady days of pursuit. Since breaking out of Normandy on August 1, the Allied armies — now over two million men with nearly half a million vehicles — had chased a desperate Wehrmacht on the run. Each Allied soldier had been treated like a celebrity as he rolled through liberated towns and villages. After caving in at Normandy, the Germans had not been able to reconstruct a front across 300 miles. The remnants of their army shuffled into POW cages by the thousands while their destroyed ordnance cluttered the roads. The once-fearsome Luftwaffe had disappeared while the skies buzzed with thousands of Allied fighters and bombers. Patton had told Omar Bradley, "Damn it, Brad, just give me 400,000 gallons of gasoline and I'll put you inside Germany in two days."

But gas and ammo were not to be had given the feeble Allied supply lines which still depended foremost on the Normandy beaches. Patton's Third Army in the south was most starved for fuel, Hodges' First Army in the center almost as much.

Montgomery and Patton both lobbied Eisenhower for priority to execute one sharp thrust across the Rhine. The German body was obviously shaken, teetering, and one heavy punch could knock it over. Eisenhower personally favored a broad front strategy, applying equal pressure on all points. But Montgomery, due to his rank, prestige and the backing of the British government, won his argument to launch a daring single thrust to propel the Allies over the Rhine. A factor in his favor was that his plan would finally re-employ the airborne divisions. The paratroopers were the toughest, best-trained infantry in the Allied armies, but they had been idle for 10 weeks and pressure had mounted to get them back in the battle.

Operation Market Garden began with the U.S. 101st and 82nd Airborne Divisions seizing a 60-mile corridor of highway and bridges to the north, while at the tip of the advance the British 1st Airborne seized a bridge over the Rhine at Arnhem. The XXX Corps attacked to flesh out the airborne corridor with armor and propel a solid thrust across the Rhine.

The 2nd Armored, faced with increasing resistance on its front, wasn't alone among U.S. divisions rooting for the daring operation to succeed. Recon troops from the 41st Armored Infantry were dispatched north towards Arnhem to feel out the situation, but soon returned with reports that the area was alive with German formations. As it turned out, the operation failed. The British 1st Airborne Division was nearly wiped out and both American airborne divisions would be pinned in Holland, fighting as infantry, until Thanksgiving. Somehow the apparent German collapse of late summer had transformed into a deadly defensive shell around the Reich. A chill swept over the front in more ways than one. The Allies were about to settle in for a long, cold winter.

THE WESTWALL

What the Germans called the "Miracle of the West" owed much to the Allied supply shortage, though it cannot be said that the Allies ever had less fuel or ammunition than the Wehrmacht. A more important factor was that by precipitously ceding France and Belgium, the Germans had shortened their Western obligations enormously, and now men and machines were close at hand, easily put into the line. Defying the damage assessments of the Allied strategic bomber chiefs, German war production reached its zenith in September 1944, and new tanks and guns no longer had to pass a tortuous network of destroyed rails and bridges, and a gauntlet of Thunderbolts and Typhoons to

Above right and below: The Westwall, or Siegfried Line, was a three-mile deep series of fortifications that included strongpoints, pillboxes, minefields and dragon's teeth anti-tank defenses such as those seen in these two photographs. That at right shows men of 9th Infantry Division on a tank of 3rd Armored.
U.S. Army via George Forty

reach the battlefront. As daylight hours shortened and Allied tactical air bases receded hundreds of miles away, the German front quickly fleshed out with new men and equipment.

But the most significant factor in stopping the Allied advance was the Westwall, or as the Allies called it, the Siegfried Line. In the late 1930s Hitler had led a massive national effort, using a third of Germany's annual concrete output, to construct a web of fortifications on the border. It consisted of massive pillboxes with interlocking fields of fire, and vast areas lined with "dragon's teeth" to defy tanks. For the Germans falling back from France, the Westwall had a psychological as well as material advantage. Finally they had a prepared line to hold. After 1940 the Westwall had been stripped of its guns and communications equipment to man the Atlantic Wall, but by fall 1944 the emplacements were still intact and new equipment was hastily reinstalled. The intervening years had covered the fortifications with grass or foliage so they were invisible from the air, sometimes nearly so from ground level.

The Westwall had an additional advantage in that it could be manned by low-grade infantry, raised quickly from the populace — in fact anyone who could pull a trigger. While Germany's elite combat troops had been forced to line the front in Normandy, behind the Westwall they could now be reserved for counterattacks. One more advantage that swung to the Germans on the Westwall was that local intelligence now worked in their favor. During the great pursuit, French and Belgian civilians had assisted the Allies, informing them of enemy locations and providing armed groups to harass the retreaters. Now that the battle had reached Germany, civilian sentiment lay with the Wehrmacht. In the fall of 1944, the 2nd Armored Division would fight its most difficult battles of the war.

In First Army's sector, the initial plan was to surround and seize the border city of Aachen. This would not only punch a hole in the Westwall but strike a blow against Hitler's prestige. After preliminary thrusts to secure the flanks, the general plan called for XIX Corps from the north and VII Corps from the south to join hands east of the city, cutting it off from reinforcement. In the last days of September, XIX Corps' artillery began shelling the Westwall. On October 2 the attack began, 2nd Armored's CCB, divided into two task forces, following the infantry of the 30th Division, whose first task was to bridge

Below: A machine-gun crew follows a 2AD tank toward Ubach during the breaching of the Westwall on October 6, 1944. *U.S. Army via Real War Photos*

the Wurm River running parallel to the front. Task Force 2, led by Col. Sidney Hinds, was first across the river, only to find the infantry had not been able to expand their bridgehead. German artillery targeted the congestion, delaying the advance by hitting vehicles on the bridges.

The next morning CCB's Task Force 1, led by Col. Paul Disney, crossed the Wurm and, finding the infantry still stalled, headed due east into a storm of enemy fire. Two tank platoons were ordered to seize high ground beyond Ubach and ran into seven German assault guns. Trading two Shermans for three of the enemy SPGs, the platoons staggered on through artillery fire but were stopped short of their objective. After dark, two companies of German infantry that tried to slip behind the task force were caught and destroyed.

By the 4th, a gap had opened up between the two task forces and the 1st Battalion, 67th Armored, and a company of 41st Armored Infantry was ordered up from CCR to fill it. The 1st Battalion met immediate resistance and by the end of the day had lost 10 tanks. The bridgehead had grown enough so that all of CCB had gotten across the Wurm, although by now the combat command had lost half its tanks. 2nd Armored's maintenance battalion was ordered to the front so that cripples wouldn't have to be towed back over the bridges.

The next day CCA, with a regiment attached from the 29th Infantry Division, entered the battle. While CCB plunged east and northeast to form a protective shield over the corps' offensive, CCA was to attack southeast in support of the 30th Division to encircle Aachen, joining hands with the 3rd Armored and 1st Infantry Divisions of VII Corps coming up from the south. CCA had both of its task forces in position for the attack on the 6th.

CCB had meanwhile continued to drive northeast to cut the roads leading from the German road and rail center of Geilenkirchen, where there was known to be a concentration of tanks. When Disney's Task Force 1 attempted to attack under a rolling artillery barrage, Panthers and Tigers suddenly appeared on the plain to their front. In the brief slugging match that followed, 21 of 34 Shermans were knocked out. The U.S. mediums were not only outgunned by the enemy tanks and had thinner frontal armor, but to the tankers' dismay, in soggy mud the Shermans even lost their advantage in speed and maneuverability. The Germans had learned earlier in Russia to equip their new tanks with wider tracks. American ingenuity responded with improvised track extenders, called "duckbills," but these usually didn't work.

Disney came up with a daring gambit. Assembling a company of light M5 tanks, he launched them at the German heavies. The Stuarts didn't sink into the mud and raced across the field at 35mph, faster than the Panzers could traverse their turrets. The light tanks got into the enemy rear where they overran an artillery battery and scoured enemy trenches with machine-gun fire. Three M5s got held up in a ditch and were destroyed, but the rest created havoc. At one point the Stuarts even took on a platoon of Tigers. Their 37mm guns were as effective as pellets against the German armor, but the speed of the M5s confounded the enemy beasts and forced them to withdraw. At this point 2nd Armored's CCB had not quite reached its objective but it had

Below: Men of 2nd Armored load 105mm shells onto an M7 HMC, on October 25, 1944, just after the fall of Aachen. The standard weapon of the armored division's artillery units, the M7 HMC had the chassis of the M3 medium, the M7B1 that of the M4. The main armament was a 105mm M1A2, M2 or M2A1 howitzer fired by a gun crew of five, bringing the total crew to seven including commander and driver. *U.S. Army via Real War Photos*

penetrated the Westwall nearly to its eastern edge. The Germans launched a massive counterattack that afternoon, but both Hinds and Disney held their ground. XIX Corps ordered CCB to go on the defensive until the issue at Aachen was decided.

To the south, Colliers' CCA with attached infantry from the 29th Division lined up to the left of 30th Division for the drive to encircle Aachen. Crossing its start-line on the morning of October 5, CCA ran into a torrent of fire from interlocking bunkers and artillery. Progress was measured by yards, the Germans defending "each grubby village," in Bradley's words, "like it was the Brandenburg Gate." After two days of twisting itself into the German defense belt, CCA had extended its line to connect with CCB's defenses to the left. The 2nd Armored was being pummeled by German artillery to the east, much of it out of range of U.S. artillery still behind the Wurm.

Above: An M8 assault gun of the 3rd Battalion, 67th Armored, moves past the railway station in Palenberg, Germany on October 4, 1944. At Palenberg, 2nd Armored established a bridgehead over the Wurm River on its first breach of the Westwall. The M8 was built on the chassis of the M5 light and provided a close-support howitzer that equipped HQ companies of medium tank battalions until replaced by the 105mm-equipped M4. Nearly 2,000 M8s were produced between the end of 1942 and January 1944.
U.S. Army via Real War Photos

VII Corps was having similar problems, so both the northern and southern prongs of the U.S. pincer halted to consolidate their positions. Aachen itself was defended by only four weak divisions, two of them hastily raised Volkssturm, but Field Marshal Model was trying to assemble a counterattack force of four Panzer divisions.

The U.S. attack resumed on October 13, the 30th and 1st Infantry Divisions forming the inside of the pincers while the 2nd and 3rd Armored Divisions formed the outer ring. In the brutal fighting that followed Captain James Burt earned the Hell on Wheels' second Medal of Honor. (See page 87.)

On October 16 XIX Corps and VII Corps completed the encirclement of Aachen. CCA took up defensive positions against German counterattacks, while a great drama played out inside the pocket. Hitler had ordered that the ancient city — already reduced to rubble by Allied air — be defended to the death. But though the German defenders resisted desperately in street to street fighting, on October 21 the city's last commander surrendered. "When the Americans start using 155s as sniper weapons," he remarked, "it is time to give in."

With the conquest of Aachen the Allies had made their first significant breach in the Westwall. 2nd Armored's CCA was pulled into divisional reserve, and the division as a whole licked its wounds. Battle casualties on the Siegfried Line had been 899 (126 killed) with over 1,000 non-battle casualties and 211 cases of combat fatigue. At this time the 2nd Armored became part of William H. Simpson's Ninth Army. After concluding the siege of Brest on the Atlantic coast, Ninth Army had been inserted into the Ardennes sector, but Bradley suspected that Montgomery would soon ask for U.S. troops to reinforce his command. In order to keep his First Army away from Monty's grasp, Bradley inserted the Ninth Army next to the British. 2nd Armored and XIX Corps formed the veteran core of Ninth Army, which otherwise consisted of new or relatively untested divisions. At this time, too, Charles Corlett was sent back to the States for rest and recuperation and XIX Corps was given to Raymond S. McLain.

**2nd ARMORED UNITs
as organised July 26–31, 1944**

Combat Command A

CO Brigadier General Maurice Rose

HQ CCA

66th Armd Regt

22nd RCT (w/normal attachments)

14th Armd Fd Arty Bn

Cos A, C, & Det Co E, 17th Armd Engr Bn

702nd TD Bn (SP) (less Co B)

Co A, 48th Armd Med Bn

Det Maint Bn

Bty D, 195th AAA (AW) Bn (SP)

Combat Command B

CO Brigadier General I.D. White

HQ CCB

67th Armd Regt (less 3rd Bn)

1st & 3rd Bns, 41st Armd Inf Regt

78th Armd Fd Arty Bn

Co B & Det Co E, 17th Armd Engr Bn

Co B, 702nd TD Bn

Co B, 48th Armd Med Bn

Bty A, 195th AAA (AW) Bn (SP)

502nd CIC Det (2 Officers, 14 enlisted
  Men)

Division Reserve

41st Armd Inf Regt (-1st and 3rd Bns)

3rd Bn, 67th Armd Regt, (-I Company)

Division Control

HQ & HQ Co (with 1 Co, 41st Armd Inf Div
  attached plus 3 sections, Bty C, 195th
  AAA (AW) Bn (SP)

142nd Armd Sig Co, 82nd Armd Recon Bn
  (+Co D, 17th Armd Engr Bn)

24th Recon Sqn, Mech (-1 Troop)

Division Trains (plus Bty B, 195th AAA (AW)
  Bn (SP))

HQ 195th AAA (AW) Bn (SP)

17th Armd Engr Bn (less 5 companies)

Division Artillery

HQ Div Arty

62nd, 65th, & 92nd Fd Arty Bns

Bty C, 195th AAA (AW) Bn (SP) (less 3
  sections)

Btys C & D, 129th AAA Gun Bn (90mm)

THE ROER

After hammering a hole through the Westwall at Aachen, the U.S. high command thought that their next jump would reach the Rhine. An intervening obstacle, however, varying six to 10 miles from the Westwall and 25 to 30 miles before the Rhine, was the Roer River. The ground to the Roer was mostly flat, dotted with small villages, but heavy rains in late October and early November turned much of the ground to sticky mud. The Roer itself had grown from its usual 200 to 300 yards wide. More important, the Germans had resolved not to cede a foot of their home territory, their front had steadily fleshed out with reinforcements, and the 9th Panzer Division had crossed west of the Roer to resist the offensive.

Harmon first issued his attack plans on November 6, but since the operation called for massive air support, bad weather continually forced delays. When blue skies finally appeared on November 16, the attack kicked off. From England, 2,400 Allied bombers escorted by 1,000 fighters pulverized German positions west of the Roer. Though nearly on the scale of the carpet bombing at St. Lô, this strike was not as effective because it covered 100 square miles rather than half a dozen, and the clouds soon closed in again. 2nd Armored, flanked by the 29th and 30th Infantry Divisions, had been assigned a narrow two-mile front so that only Isaac White's CCB, divided into three task forces, made the initial attack.

Task Force 1 on the southern flank advanced against the village of Puffendorf. Wading through enemy artillery and mortar fire, the 67th Regiment tankers also struggled with the ground, losing four tanks to mud and six more to mines before reaching their objective. In the center, Task Force 2 led with its Shermans, drawing artillery fire away from the following infantry. The task force overran enemy positions in taking its first objective, Floverich, but ran into an ambush on the approaches to Apweiler. German anti-tank guns firing at close range from woods brewed up seven Shermans. Task Force 2 pulled back and went into defensive positions for the night. On the left, Task Force X lost several tanks to mines before making it to the outskirts of Immendorf.

On the first day, CCB had made good progress, destroying a full regiment of the German 183rd Division en route. But it now occupied a salient, taking enemy counterfire from three sides during the night. This prevented supplies and reinforcements from reaching the front line; even worse, between blasts of artillery, the 2AD men could hear the sound of enemy tanks moving into position.

The next day, while the two lefthand task forces joined to resume the attack on Apweiler, Col. Disney's Task Force 1, led by the 1st and 2nd Battalions, 67th Armored, advanced on Geronsweiler. The attack had barely begun when a counterattack of some 20 Panzers appeared from under the morning mist, taking the task force in flank. Artillery fire drove the infantry to ground while a pure armor battle raged on the muddy plain — one in which the Americans did not hold the advantage. The heavier weapons of the 9th Panzer Division methodically destroyed tank after tank of the 2nd Armored. Disney fell back to Puffendorf where fortunately an advance element of CCA had arrived. After six hours the Germans broke off the engagement, leaving 57 wrecked U.S. tanks on the field, half of them completely destroyed. With 366 personnel losses it was the 2nd Armored's costliest day of the war. The Germans were thought to have lost 17 tanks.

The next day Harmon committed all of CCA plus the 702nd Tank Destroyer Battalion, which had received new M36 TDs with 90mm guns. The division also borrowed a squadron of British flamethrowing tanks to uproot enemy infantry. By now elements of the 10th SS Panzer Division, the 15th Panzergrenadiers and an independent Tiger battalion were on the front. On November 20, the "Hell on Wheels" again surged toward Geronsweiler and at least 60 enemy Panzers rolled out to meet them. It was one of the biggest head-to-head tank battles fought in the west and this time the 2nd Armored held its own. At one point, a group of M5 Stuarts sallied out as a lure, and when the enemy gave chase they were impaled on the waiting 90mms of the 702nd TDs.

On November 23, Thanksgiving, Harmon gave his division half a day of rest. Aside from German defense lines, incessant counterattacks and countless minefields, the men had been drenched in freezing rain, many of them having to sleep in utter muck or foxholes full of water. The Germans, holding prepared emplacements or villages, were less effected by the elements than the attackers, who had to hold improvised positions in the open field. At this time the U.S. press began to vent outrage about the inferiority of the Sherman to German armor.

After the brief respite CCA, with a regiment from the 30th Infantry Division, attacked the fortified town of Merzenhausen, just short of the Roer. By darkness on the 24th they had seized a third of the town, but then a German counterattack led by Tigers forced them out. The next day the attack resumed and the Americans got halfway

Above: On the Roer River front in November 1944, Lt. Col. H. Hart examines a captured Königstiger (Royal Tiger) tank that was being used for ammunition testing. *Courtesy of Mark Bando*

through the town. Sometimes entrenched German infantry surrendered as soon as they saw a flamethrowing Crocodile tank come near. In the town itself, savage house-to-house fighting raged, the Germans firing down from second-story windows. On the 27th, John Collier launched CCA and its attached infantry into an all-out assault to surround and take Merzenhausen. The outcome was decided when the 3rd Battalion of 41st Armored Infantry, attacking without tank support, overran a German trench-line east of the town and then used the captured position to beat off a Panzer counterattack. Later the 2nd Battalion of the 41st came up as reinforcement and the 17th Armored Engineers, supported by 30th Division infantry, mopped up the last-ditch holdouts in Merzenhausen. Tanks were kept out of the streets because of the threat of mines, Panzerfaust and Panzerschreck (bazooka) fire. By the end of the day 337 prisoners had been taken and the town was secured.

Though enemy artillery fire remained heavy, it was seen that the Germans had finally begun to pull their forward elements back across the Roer. The 2nd Armored's last objective on the west bank, the river village of Barmen, was occupied on November 29.

It had taken the 2nd Armored 13 days to gain less than 10 miles, at a cost of 1,505 battle casualties (203 killed, 1,104 wounded and 198 missing). As the days grew shorter and the weather worsened, the Rhine began to look farther away than ever.

Elsewhere on the broad front, the situation was no better. The Canadian First Army had lost 16,000 men in backtracking to seize the Schelde Estuary. British Second Army was bogged down in Holland. Patton's Third Army was still grappling with tenacious German resistance around Metz. The worst travail, however, was undergone by First Army in the Hürtgen Forest, or what U.S. soldiers called the "Forest of Hell."

As both U.S. armor and infantry bludgeoned their way yard by yard to the Roer, the Germans held on to a trump in two massive dams upstream (south) of Aachen. In early November, the 28th Infantry had nearly reached the dams but was beaten back by vicious counterattacks around the village of Schmidt. Since then, three infantry divisions had been fed into the inferno of the Hürtgen, which stretched between Aachen and the dams.

The Germans had two options with the dams: they could wait for U.S. spearheads to cross the Roer and then blow them completely, releasing a short but devastating flash flood to wipe away bridges and material. Or they could destroy only the sluices, creating a gradual, widening inundation of the river that would postpone any U.S. offensives for weeks. Allied aircraft tried to wrest this Damocles sword from the Germans by breaking the dams themselves, but they were only partially successful and November rains made up the difference. Meanwhile, a succession of U.S. infantry divisions were fed into the meatgrinder of the Hürtgen Forest in the direction of the dams.

With the exception of the penetration into Germany the 2nd Armored had helped to achieve around Aachen, the opposing lines looked much the same as they had in 1940. Allied armies had closed up to the German border while both sides seemed unwilling — or in the Germans' case, unable — to launch strategic offenses. In the north the U.S. Ninth and First Armies threatened the Ruhr industrial region while Patton's Third Army threatened the Saar. In between was the hilly Ardennes, a forest region straddling Luxembourg and Belgium, which was considered a quiet sector by both sides. The Americans sent divisions that had been mangled in the Hürtgen, like the 2nd and 28th Infantry Divisions, to the Ardennes to rest and recuperate. They also used the region to acclimate novice divisions, like the 9th Armored, and 99th and 106th Infantry. On the other side the Germans appeared to do the same, manning their part, called the Eifel, with new conscript divisions, called Volksgrenadiers or Volkssturm, the latter consisting of misfits, older men and boys.

During November, Allied intelligence had become aware that Hitler had assembled a new Sixth Panzer Army which, along with the Fifth Panzer Army, was poised near Cologne to contest any Allied drive to the Rhine. This was bad news for the 2nd Armored Division, which was due to spearhead that inevitable U.S. assault. On December 15, First Army launched still another attack against the Roer dams. But the next morning brought bigger news. The Sixth and Fifth Panzer Armies had suddenly appeared out of nowhere to shatter the American front in the Ardennes. The inventors of Blitzkrieg were once again driving west, threatening to unhinge the entire Allied front.

THE BATTLE OF THE BULGE

Hitler had first planned the Ardennes Offensive even as German armies were retreating from their broken front in Normandy. He intended it as a grand counterstroke that would crash through the weakest sector of the American front, turn northwest across the Meuse in the rear of U.S. First Army and the British 21st Army Group, and finally seize the port of Antwerp. The German commanders charged with executing the offensive thought they would be lucky to reach the Meuse at all. Nevertheless, Sepp Dietrich, commanding Sixth Panzer Army, and Hasso von Manteuffel, commanding the Fifth, put all their expertise into the attack. They were helped during the first week by weather that grounded the Allied air forces, and by the fact that they were able to achieve surprise.

At first the U.S. high command was stunned, having not believed the Germans were still capable of such an offensive. But the U.S. soon made up for its hesitation with mobility, dispatching forces to line the penetration. Aside from armored divisions, the U.S. had 40 independent tank battalions attached to infantry on the broad front, and enough transport so that any infantry division could be motorized at any time. The threat against Liège — a mammoth Allied supply depot — and then Antwerp was gradually perceived, and reinforcements from First and Ninth Armies were rushed to deny the Germans the north, forcing the bulge to spread west.

By December 19 the magnitude of the German counteroffensive — at first obscured by lack of air reconnaissance and broken communications — had become clear to the Allied high command. The 2nd Armored was put on alert to move within six hours' notice. The next morning it was replaced in the line by the 29th Infantry Division and pulled into Ninth Army reserve. A few hours later it was attached to First Army's VII Corps. Coincidentally or not, this move would reunite the 2nd Armored Division with the 3rd Armored in a corps led by Lightning Joe Collins — the same winning combination that had cracked the German front in Normandy.

December 20 also saw Bradley lose his control of First and Ninth Armies. His 12th Army Group headquarters now commanded only Patton's Third. All forces to the north of the bulge were now under Montgomery's command.

On December 21, the 2nd Armored prepared to move some 100 miles to the west. As darkness fell, Harmon asked his chief of staff, Col. Clayton Mansfield, when they could get started. Mansfield prudently replied at 5:00 the next morning. Harmon barked that they had to move immediately, but he was informed that they didn't have any maps. It was settled to begin the march at 11:00 that night.

The division moved in two columns, preceded by the 82nd Recon Battalion, which dropped off guides and MPs at crossroads. Observing radio silence and blackout conditions, the 2AD made steady progress through the night and next day. In this remarkable march over icy roads, only 30 out of nearly 3,000 vehicles failed, and the last elements of the division had pulled into assembly areas south of Huy, Belgium, by midnight on the 22nd.

At the same time, the recon battalion of 2nd Armored's old acquaintance, the 2nd Panzer Division, pulled into Celles, due south of Huy, just four miles from the Meuse. 2nd Panzer was the spearhead of Fifth Panzer Army, and had made the deepest penetration of any German division in the Bulge. To its right and slightly behind, the 116th Panzer Division was battling the U.S. 84th Infantry Division for the crossroads town of Marche. The Panzer Lehr Division, after dropping off a regiment to help at Bastogne, was pulling up on 2nd Panzer's left.

On the 23rd, 2AD patrols probed south and one led by Lt. Everett Jones ran into tanks just south of the town of Ciney. Jones was wounded and his armored car destroyed, but he managed to get back to division HQ to report the enemy presence. Harmon was having lunch when Jones came in with a bloody bandage around his head. Harmon went outside and buttonholed a tank company commander to ask how long it would take him to get started. The man replied five minutes if he could break radio silence. Harmon figured that by now the enemy was aware of 2AD's presence and ordered him to forget about silence, just get to Ciney and "Start fighting. The whole damn division is coming right behind you."

CCA's Task Force A drove 10 miles south to Ciney, which was unoccupied, then headed southeast to Buissonville, which was held by 2nd Panzer. Task Force B followed up, and after dark CCA spread cautiously along the road net, on the alert for Germans.

At one point F Company of the 41st Armored Infantry was probing south, the men on foot followed by their halftracks, when they heard an approaching vehicle column. Captain George Bonney signaled his men to take cover on either side of the road as a German convoy, led by

Below: Men of 2nd Armored's 41st Armored Infantry during the Battle of the Bulge. This photo was apparently taken before proper winter clothing reached the division on January 11, 1945.
Courtesy of Mark Bando

captured U.S. jeeps, trucks and an ambulance passed through. The company opened fire, joined by the .50-cal. machine-guns from its halftracks. All 12 vehicles on the road went up in flames and 30 Germans were killed, an equal number captured. The only mishap was that, after Bonney had ordered everyone to cease fire, one last burst from a U.S. halftrack badly wounded him in the leg.

Just as CCA groped its way in the dark southeast toward Buissonville, the leading battle group of 2nd Panzer had progressed due west, arriving at Celles, just a short jump from Dinant on the Meuse. (The town where Rommel's 7th Panzer had crossed the Meuse in 1940.) But the German battle group and its recon element had advanced so fast that a gap had opened between it and the rest of the division, and the lead Panzers were nearly out of gas.

On Christmas Eve, 2nd Panzer's recon battalion advanced even farther, to the village of Foy-Nôtre-Dame just three miles from Dinant. A column thrust onward to the river but was surprised by British tanks posted on the east side of the Meuse. This contingent of five Shermans from 3rd Royal Tank Regiment had been ordered to guard the approaches to the bridge, and if the worst should happen, arrange their tanks to form a roadblock while engineers blew the bridge. After shooting up two tanks and a German ammunition truck, causing a spectacular explosion, the British pulled back to the bridge to contemplate their upcoming suicide stand. 2nd Panzer recon, however, also pulled back to Foy-Nôtre-Dame to wait for reinforcements.

That day, 2nd Armored's CCB pulled into Ciney, preparing to attack southwest against the Germans nearest the Meuse. The division's armored field artillery battalions took up firing positions. CCA continued southeast toward Buissonville and Rochefort, looking to chop the enemy spearhead off at the neck. As Task Force A fought its way through enemy armored outposts into Buissonville, Task Force B occupied the surrounding heights. In the afternoon, some 41st Regiment troops climbed a ridge from which they could see a huge German column heading for the town. Word went out to the 14th AFA Battalion to open fire on the target. When the Germans scattered, the spotters on the ridge were able to direct artillery fire to chase them into the woods. Left behind on the road were 36 destroyed vehicles and 10 guns. The 2AD accepted 108 surrenders.

Though CCA was already engaged with the enemy, Harmon had still not received permission to attack, and what followed was an almost comedic exchange. Montgomery had met with First Army commander Courtney Hodges the day before and stated his intent to go on the defensive along the entire northern flank of the Bulge. To this end he had ordered the liquidation of the "fortified goose egg," a salient near St. Vith held by the 82nd Airborne, parts of the 3rd, 7th, and 9th Armored Divisions, and elements of other units. Monty thought the Germans were preparing another heavy blow and he wanted to straighten and shorten the front through withdrawals. He authorized the 2nd Armored to retreat to a line between the towns of Andenne and Hotton.

When Harmon called VII Corps, Lightning Joe Collins was away but the corps artillery commander, Williston Palmer, relayed the request to First Army's chief of staff, William Kean. Speaking carefully over the radio, Kean told Palmer to look on his map for two

Above: In January 1945, during the Battle of the Bulge, 2nd Armored men operate their 81mm mortar from the rear of an M4A1 halftrack. A purpose-built mortar-carrying version of the M2, over 1,000 of the M4 and improved M4A1 (with strengthened floor to allow onboard use of mortar) versions were built.
U.S. Army via Real War Photos

Right: Two views of M4s in the brutal winter conditions that prevailed during the Battle of the Bulge. *U.S. Army via George Forty*

towns beginning with A and H, meaning Andenne and Hotton, 30 miles in 2nd Armored's rear. Palmer looked at his map and instead saw two tiny villages, Achêne and le Houisse, to 2nd Armored's front. He enthusiastically said he understood the orders. Kean grew suspicious and called back to clarify the directive. By that time Collins, who like most senior First Army officers resented being put under Monty's command, had met personally with Harmon. The key was that Monty had "authorized" a withdrawal, not specifically ordered it. With no fewer than four Panzer divisions closing in on the Meuse, the 2nd Armored would attack.

At dawn on Christmas Day, CCA drove southeast toward Rochefort, briefly held by men from the 84th Infantry Division, only to meet elements of Panzer Lehr coming the other way. An intervening village, Humain, had briefly been held by cavalry troops attached to the 2AD, but they, too, were driven out by the Germans. CCA counterattacked the village without success, but in turn thwarted a German attack on Buissonville. By the end of the day, CCA was also grappling with lead elements of 9th Panzer, which had entered the Bulge on December 22. The important thing was that now an armored blocking line stood between the Germans and the Meuse, and CCA had bought time for CCB to destroy 2nd Panzer's spearheads that had neared the river.

CCB's Christmas attack was aimed southwest toward Celles, where the lead battlegroup of the 2nd Panzer had been isolated near the Meuse. Celles lay between two ridgelines and Task Force B circled right to gain one, while Task Force A swerved left to occupy the other. The area was heavily wooded and both columns took heavy fire from concealed German positions along the roads. The day was clear and the skies were swarming with Allied fighter-bombers. Held up by a platoon of Panthers, Task Force B called for P-38 Lightnings to blast the fireblock. Once flushed out of their positions, the enemy tanks were destroyed. After CCB gained the ridges, the town of Celles fell easily. The main strength of the enemy battlegroup, however, still held out in woods to the north.

That night both 2nd Panzer and Panzer Lehr tried to reinforce 2nd Panzer's isolated battlegroup. At dawn on the 26th the two German columns faced intervening heights full of 2AD tanks and massed U.S. artillery fire. CCB summoned squadrons of Typhoons to pound the Germans before they could form up for attack. The Germans withdrew their reinforcement columns and eventually authorized 2nd Panzer's forward battlegroup to break back to the lines. About 600 men snuck out between 2nd Armored outposts on foot. Left behind were some 550 dead, 1,203 prisoners, 82 armored vehicles, just as many guns, and hundreds of other vehicles, many of them abandoned for lack of gas.

2nd Armored's 82nd Recon Battalion had spent Christmas Day swooping down on the right of CCB to encircle its counterpart, the recon battalion of 2nd Panzer, which was holed up at Foy-Nôtre-Dame. 82nd Recon coordinated its attack with the 3rd Royal Tanks, who had formerly guarded the Meuse crossing and were now advancing with reinforcements northeast. The first meeting between Allies turned awkward when an American tank destroyed the first British one it saw. But the German recon troops were surrounded and their survivors, 148 men, surrendered. 2nd Panzer's recon battalion, which had made the farthest advance of any German troops in the Battle of the Bulge, had been removed permanently from the war.

It is interesting to note that prior to 2nd Armored's attack, the British guarding the Dinant bridge had seen an American jeep racing up the road alongside the river. The British had planted mines across the road and tried to warn the jeep, but its occupants didn't understand and it was blown apart. When the British investigated the three bodies they found German soldiers wearing American overcoats. This incident is usually attributed to Otto Skorzeny's infamous operation that inserted English-speaking commandos behind the U.S. lines, but it is just as likely the men were members of 2nd Panzer's recon battalion. In any case, some Germans did reach the Meuse.

Below: This squad of 2AD's 82nd Recon Battalion was cut off behind the lines for three days during the Battle of the Bulge, but as shown here, they were able to liberate a side of beef from a horsedrawn German supply wagon. On the left (sporting a Luger) is James W. Provens. The three men on the right are Louis Pilotti, Nick Palazonis, and Sgt. Carl Boettinger, with the BAR. *Photo courtesy of Timothy Provens*

While 2nd Armored's CCB was obliterating the German spearhead, CCA continued to beat back German attacks from Humain. The enemy likewise defied CCA's thrusts from Buissonville. Finally, after the Germans in Humain had been pummeled by a day and night of artillery fire, CCR moved in on the 27th to launch a five-pronged attack. The Germans resisted with ferocity and at the end it took a flamethrowing tank to compel the last hold-outs to surrender. It is possible that 2nd Panzer clung to Humain so desperately in order to retrieve more remnants of its forward battlegroup. After the 27th, 2nd Panzer and Panzer Lehr pulled back, leaving 9th Panzer to oppose any further 2AD assaults.

Having defied Montgomery's intentions with its Christmas attack, if not his specific orders, the "Hell on Wheels" now became part of the defensive regrouping on the northern flank. In fact, at this point, the entire Battle of the Bulge shifted its axis.

In the last days of December Hitler acknowledged that his original plan — a northwest thrust across the Meuse toward Antwerp — was no longer possible. The Bulge had been hammered by U.S. divisions on the northern flank into an incursion due west, where no important objectives lay, and in any case the westerly spearhead of the offensive had just been crushed by the unexpected appearance of the 2nd Armored Division.

Hitler now had two options: to withdraw completely from the salient, thus saving men and equipment for the future; or to continue tying down nearly all of Bradley's 12th Army Group plus half of Montgomery's forces (held in reserve) in a battle on ground of his choosing. He chose the latter option, switching the focus of the German effort to Patton's build-up around Bastogne. Though the crossroads town was no longer important for a drive to the Meuse, it presented the opportunity to diminish U.S. forces in winter warfare, in which the Germans would optimally hold the strategic offensive but tactical defensive. Hitler ordered I SS Panzer Corps to move from Dietrich's Sixth Panzer Army to Manteuffel's Fifth in the south. In the north, Montgomery could be relied upon for caution; no immediate counteroffensive was expected in that quarter.

In the last days of December, the men of 2nd Armored enjoyed a belated Christmas dinner and then a New Year's one of turkey. The 67th Armored Regiment also organized a New Year's dance, though a disappointing number of females showed up.

On the southern flank of the Bulge, ferocious fighting took place between Third Army and elements of the First with Fifth Panzer Army, now reinforced by the I SS Panzer Corps. In the north, front-line troops on both sides fought amidst brutal winter conditions while U.S. forces were gathered for a decisive counterattack. It is a matter of debate whether the Allies should have tried to cut the Germans off in the Ardennes; as it stands, their first objective was the town of Houffalize, in the center of the Bulge.

When Montgomery's counteroffensive started up on January 3, it featured an impressive array of U.S. firepower. The two "heavy" armored divisions in the U.S. order of battle — the 2nd and 3rd — were now side by side, the "Hell on Wheels" flanked by the 84th Infantry Division on its right and the 3rd Armored flanked by the 83rd Infantry on its left. In snowstorms and sub-zero darkness that fell at 4:30, the attack ran into fierce German resistance. Tanks were confined to the roads, which were covered by anti-tank guns in ambush position. For every 500 yards gained,

Below: A 2nd Armored Sherman knocked out around Celles in December 1944. In this photo one can recognize how U.S. tanks attacking in the open could be surprised by Panzers concealed within the tree-line. *Courtesy of Mark Bando*

Above: M4 during the Bulge.
U.S. Army via George Forty

an enemy counterattack would regain 200. German tanks contested small hamlets, as much for the warmth they represented as for strategic advantage.

After four days, the 2nd Armored had gained four miles at the cost of 400 casualties. (3rd Armored's gains and losses were almost identical.) 2AD's coordination with the 84th Infantry Division — which had been living in foxholes for three weeks — was less than desired; nevertheless one 84th private, Roscoe Blunt, paid tribute to the tankers: "I recall seeing and hearing through the fog the vicious tank battles. Afterward we saw the aftermath, the losses, observing each body slumped over a turret or burning on the ground beside their 'steel coffin.' Infantrymen had sort of a strange love affair with the tank boys. We admired their bravery. On the other hand, we felt sort of sorry for them for too often we saw them being incinerated — to us a most horrible way to die. Our ways of dying were bad enough. It was sort of like the police officer–firefighter relationship."

On January 7, Montgomery gave his famous press conference in which he called the Bulge "one of the trickiest" battles he had ever "handled." Bradley, Patton, Collins and other American commanders were so incensed that Churchill had to intervene, calling the Bulge an "American battle."

That day, the 2nd Armored began an assault on Samree, a crossroads village atop a height that commanded the surrounding area. Colonel Clayton Mansfield, Harmon's chief of staff, had just been assigned to command the 66th Armored Regiment, and went forward to survey the ground. A German artillery shot killed him. On the night of January 8, divisional artillery poured 12,500 rounds into Samree and over the next two days both CCA and CCB ground their way within 1,000 yards of the village from the east and west. On the 11th a two-pronged lunge finally seized the town. That day, too, the 2nd Armored finally received a supply of winter overcoats.

January 12 marked another turn in the battle as the Soviet Red Army launched a huge offensive from the line of the Vistula River in Poland. Hitler ordered the I and II SS Panzer Corps and Dietrich's Sixth Panzer Army headquarters to withdraw from the Bulge for transfer to the east. Though the remaining German units in the Ardennes were not yet authorized to fall back, Manteuffel took his own measures to preserve Fifth Panzer Army, pulling his Panzer divisions into reserve and taking other steps to make sure troops were

U.S. "HEAVY" ARMORED DIVISION

Men:	14,500
Tanks:	232 medium, 158 light
Halftracks:	640
Artillery:	54 SP 105mm HMCs
	18 M4 105mm
	14 M8 75mm HMCs
Armd cars:	54
Other motor vehicles:	1,242

not left in the lurch without reason. The 2nd Armored noticed a steep decline of German strength on its front, though the elements and terrain remained as formidable as ever.

On the 14th the 2AD advanced three miles, its largest one-day gain in the offensive. At one point Captain James Burt, who had won the Medal of Honor at Aachen, led his company of 66th Armored tanks onto a hill from which they blasted apart a roadblock of dug-in tanks. On the next day, 2nd Armored completed a ring around Houffalize and by evening patrols had scouted the town.

On January 16, while firing still continued on the outskirts and from German rearguards, Col. Hugh O'Farrell led CCA's spearhead, a battalion of the 41st Armored Infantry, into Houffalize. While a newsreel cameraman took pictures of the men, some figures emerged cautiously from a nearby wood. They were led by Lt. Col. Miles Foy of the 41st Armored Cavalry Recon Squadron of the 11th Armored Division, part of Patton's Third Army. When Foy asked to see an officer he said, "Well Jesus Christ, if it isn't O'Farrell!" The two men had been classmates at the Armored School at Fort Knox. With this link-up between the First and Third Armies, the Bulge had been severed.

It later turned out that Patton, on learning that the 2nd Armored was on the edge of Houffalize, ordered his cavalry squadron to drive through the night to effect the link-up. They had left a nine-mile gap between themselves and any other units of Third Army.

In the January fighting, the 2nd Armored took 1,742 prisoners (two-thirds from the 560th Volksgrenadiers) and destroyed 51 tanks and SP guns. In the Bulge as a whole, 2AD suffered 201 dead, 1,165 wounded and 134 missing, 80 percent of the casualties coming after January 3. The division also suffered 1,337 non-battle casualties. Of the armored divisions in the Bulge, only the 3rd suffered more killed and wounded than "Hell on Wheels". After cutting the Bulge at Houffalize, the 2nd Armored was pulled out of the line. On January 19, Ernest Harmon was promoted once again to corps command and this time he accepted. The division passed to CCB's commander, Brig. General Isaac White. Colonel Sidney Hinds took over CCB.

Historians have debated ever since whether the Germans' Ardennes Offensive was a foolish waste of their remaining strength in the west, or an astute thrust that seriously disrupted the Allies' carefully laid plans. In the end, the Germans did not get close to their stated objectives of Liège and Antwerp, but they did dissolve Allied pressure, albeit temporarily, against the Saar and the Ruhr. First Army, Third Army, eight divisions from Ninth Army, plus Britain's most powerful formation, XXX Corps (which Monty kept in reserve), all halted their pressure on the German border. There was also the possibility that lightning could have struck, if the

Below: A 66th Armored Regiment Sherman at Tueyen, Holland on February 22, 1945, the day before Montgomery launched Operation Plunder, his spectacular crossing of the Rhine.
U.S. Army via Real War Photos

Americans had been a bit slower, or if the cloud-cover had remained a little longer. Since the walls were closing in on the Reich anyway, Hitler's final offensive, as slim a gamble as it was, was probably worth taking.

THE RHINE

After playing its lead role in the Battle of the Bulge, the 2nd Armored returned to XIX Corps, part of Ninth Army, at its former positions on the Roer north of Aachen. Unfortunately, though First Army had reverted to Bradley's control, Simpson's Ninth Army remained attached to the British 21st Army Group, which considered it little but a flanking force for its own ambitions farther north.

In order to close up to the Rhine, Montgomery planned a joint operation, Veritable and Grenade. Veritable, which kicked off on February 8, consisted of a massive British–Canadian drive from Holland toward the southeast. Grenade would follow on the 10th with Ninth Army crossing the Roer and turning northeast to join the British in a united front along the Rhine from Cologne to Wesel, just opposite the Ruhr. To enable Grenade, U.S. V Corps launched another drive to seize the Roer dams. Just like the previous attempts to reach the dams, however, this one stalled. First Army poured in more troops, including the 82nd Airborne and 9th Infantry Divisions, but when the dams finally came within sight, the Germans simply destroyed the sluices. Instead of opting for a short but devastating flash flood, they chose a gradual, unstoppable inundation of the Roer plain.

2nd Armored's role in the offensive had to be postponed for two weeks. During that period, the British Veritable attack made only slow progress through sloughs of mud and stiff German resistance. Though the delay was excruciating to U.S. commanders, the men of 2nd Armored, now with over a month off from combat, enjoyed three-day leaves while the division trained its replacements and refurbished its equipment. Another advantage of the delay was that the British attack in the north gradually drew off most of the Germans' strength. When Grenade finally got underway on February 23, it kicked off with a bang.

XIX Corps lined up the 29th and 30th Infantry Divisions to cross the Roer, supported by nearly 30 massed artillery battalions. 2nd Armored was held in reserve to exploit gains, which were not long in coming. When the artillery opened up at 3:30 a.m. on the 23rd, German counterbattery fire was almost nonexistent. The infantry crossed the Roer, methodically taking village after village. XIX Corps soon began to outpace its neighboring corps on the right, and on the 25th, 2nd Armored's CCB was ordered into the gap. Despite losing three tanks to a hit-and-run Panzer thrust, CCB met little resistance.

On the 27th, Simpson decided that the exploitation phase had arrived and inserted the "Hell on Wheels" into the center of XIX Corps. The division was augmented with attached artillery, mine-rolling and flamethrowing tanks, AA batteries, and a regiment of 83rd Division infantry, until its total strength was about double that of a standard U.S. armored division.

On the first day the attack flowed for 10 miles through a multitude of small towns or hamlets, some of them unmarked on maps. The spottiness of German resistance added to the confusion because an ambush could spring from nowhere, while obvious strongpoints had been abandoned. For example, when CCB had passed through the town of Hemmerden German Panzers emerged from a wood in their rear. Tanks from the Maintenance Battalion fended them off while fighter-bombers were called in to deliver the killing blows.

On March 1, the 2nd Armored closed up on the Nord Canal, a narrow but deep channel that served as an effective anti-tank ditch. Retreating Germans were also heading for the canal and resistance from the other side began to stiffen. The situation in

Above: "Pee Wee" Reed of the 2nd Battalion, 41st Armored Infantry, performs one of the less glamorous tasks in 1945 Germany. Note the combat leadership stripe below his chevron and the "overseas bars" worn on his tanker jacket. *Courtesy of Mark Bando*

Right: Note the paraphernalia on this M5, including logs meant to assist with crossing boggy ground as well as provide extra protection.
U.S. Army via Real War Photos

Below right: 2nd Armored rolls through Krefeld, Germany on March 3, 1945, the day that the division nearly seized an intact bridge across the Rhine. German tank and infantry hold-outs in Krefeld had tried to buy time for fellow units to escape across the river. The unit markings on the right front of the leading vehicle (2Δ67Δ) that show it is part of the 2nd Armored's 67th Armored Regiment. Note the sandbag protection (held on by chicken wire) against anti-tank weapons. *U.S. Army via Real War Photos*

Below: Reconnaissance vehicles of the division pause in Altenahr, Germany, on March 9, 1945.
U.S. Army via Real War Photos

the rear remained confused as snipers lingered in villages and 2AD's supply columns ran into ambushes. At the city of Krefeld, M5s from the 66th Armored's Recon Company came around a corner and found eight of their men standing in the street with their hands up. The tankers threw smoke grenades to allow their comrades to escape.

Seizing some bridges intact, and with the 17th Engineer Battalion laying more, 2AD surmounted the Nord Canal obstacle. By now both the Americans and Germans were trying to reach the Rhine. A company of the 41st Armored Infantry found itself in the path of a retreating column from Panzer Lehr. After a furious firefight in the dark early morning hours of March 2, the Germans broke through, leaving behind eight burning U.S. armored vehicles. A column of CCA suddenly topped a ridge and lost nine tanks to German anti-tank guns and Panzers, which then quickly retreated.

Krefeld, five miles short of the Rhine bridge at Uerdingen, became the focal point of enemy resistance. Panthers guarded the city's main street and a company of Shermans from CCA, a platoon advancing on each side, gradually hammered them out of town. Infantry fighting moved block by block. At one point a squad leader in the 66th Armored's Recon Company went down wounded. His squad scattered except for Private Charles Coons, who kept an eye on the wounded corporal. That night he snuck across the street and gunned down two Germans from behind with his Thompson submachine gun. He dragged the wounded man into a house but Germans tossed a grenade inside. Coons grabbed the grenade and threw it out the window, following it with a burst from his Tommy gun that destroyed an enemy machine-gun team. He then saw a three-man Panzerschreck team moving into position and mowed them down before they could fire. Finally another squad of Germans came into the house and Coons covered himself and the wounded corporal in a rug. The enemy soldiers came into the room and stood within arms' length of the hidden Americans, but fortunately left after a few minutes. By the next morning the town had been cleared and Coons enlisted civilians to carry the corporal to an aid station.

On that same night, Sidney Hinds' CCB had received new orders. Divisional intelligence had learned that the Rhine bridge at Uerdingen was still intact. This news went all the way up to XIX Corps headquarters, and Gen. McLain attached a regiment of the 95th Infantry Division to CCB. During the day on March 2, Hinds found a company of amphibious DUKWs, and asked for them to be attached to his command. XIX Corps contacted Montgomery to request an airborne drop to secure the far side of the bridge. Both requests were refused. Montgomery was planning his own set-piece crossing of the Rhine, and had no wish for the freelancing Americans of the 2nd Armored to steal his thunder.

Nevertheless, by late on March 2, CCB was already on the approaches to the bridge. They might have rushed it except a contingent of Dutch SS suddenly intervened. Throughout the next day, 2AD uprooted the SS house by house, until by 5:30 the bridge was once again clear. During the fight, 2nd Armored artillery had bombarded the far side with air-burst shells to keep German engineers from laying demolitions.

After darkness, Hinds dispatched a company of the 379th Infantry to scout the bridge, which was 65 feet wide and over 1,600 feet long. They went about a fifth of the way across before reporting back that they had found obstacles for tanks. While Hinds pondered this, an explosion shook the bridge. But whatever demolitions the Germans had set failed, and a patrol reported they had only blown a 13-foot hole in the roadway. 2AD's 17th Engineer Battalion was canvassed for volunteers, and 13 men crept across the bridge with orders to cut the remaining demolition wires. They went all the way to the other side and just before midnight reported back that they hadn't found any wires. Furthermore, they said the bridge was suitable for an infantry attack.

Hinds decided to send a battalion of the 379th Infantry (95th Division) and two companies of 41st Armored Infantry across. The latter were late in arriving so he allowed the 379th to send out another patrol. These men reported that the bridge was impassable and their battalion commander cancelled his participation in the attack.

Daylight on March 4 arrived with 2nd Armored's CCB staring in frustration at a nearly intact bridge across the Rhine. The Germans solved the problem at 7:00, however, when they finally blew the bridge. The center of the span collapsed into the water and with it went the opportunity for 2nd Armored to have changed the entire course of the war.

One effect of Ninth Army's successful push to the Rhine was to unhinge German resistance farther north, where the British–Canadian forces also reached the river. Not to be outdone, Bradley had ordered his First and Third Armies forward to make similar gains in the south. Compared to the vicious slugging match the "Hell on Wheels" had engaged in to reach the Roer, the drive to the Rhine was faster and less costly. Due to the proximity of German escape routes on the bridges before they were blown, the prisoner bag was modest by 2AD standards. During Operation Grenade, the 2nd Armored suffered 414 casualties including 90 killed, while capturing 2,500 Germans, killing some 900 others and destroying 37 enemy tanks.

ON TO THE ELBE

The final two months of the war were characterized by an urgent shift in German attention to the east. While the Allies had arrived at the Rhine in western Germany, a mammoth Russian army group had bulled its way to the Oder River, less than 40 miles from Berlin. All that remained for this sledgehammer to land its final blow was for the Soviets to move up their logistics and restock with ammunition. Henceforth, the nature of German resistance in the west would be mixed. Parts of the Wehrmacht would continue to follow orders fanatically, fighting to the death; others (and perhaps most civilians) were resigned to losing the war and actually wished the Anglo-Americans onward so that they and not the Russians would occupy Germany. A third category consisted of men grimly determined to protect the backs of their soldiers in the east, prolonging the war to gain time for more refugees to escape the embraces of the Red Army.

During March 1945, Montgomery perfected his plans for Operation Plunder, his extravagant offensive to cross the Rhine. In a slight embarrassment to Monty, the U.S. 9th Armored Division had grabbed a Rhine bridge at Remagen on March 9. A delighted Omar Bradley immediately expanded the bridgehead with two corps. On the 22nd, Patton slipped his 5th Infantry Division over

an unguarded part of the river, following it up with the 4th Armored. Patton's glee at crossing the Rhine one day before his rival, Montgomery, was unsurpassed.

Operation Plunder, employing two airborne divisions, hundreds of amphibious vehicles and three full armies, was the most powerful Allied offensive since D-Day. But despite a few hours of brisk fighting from German defenders, it largely hit thin air. The 2nd Armored — in fact, all of Ninth Army — was held in reserve, though on the second day of the offensive, 2AD's 17th Armored Engineer Battalion built a 1,150-foot treadway bridge in seven hours, a record time.

The 2nd Armored began to cross the river on March 28 and wasn't completely over until the 31st. The problem was that Monty was giving his British troops 19 hours a day on the bridges, leaving only five for Ninth Army, despite the fact that U.S. engineers constructed most of the bridges. On the plus side, Bradley had coordinated the breakouts from his bridgeheads with Operation Plunder and the Allies soon reassembled their full broad front east of the Rhine. Eisenhower now assumed direct control of the campaign and assigned Monty's Canadian and British armies to flanking operations in the north. The immediate objective was Germany's industrial heart, the Ruhr, and the attack would be prosecuted by First Army, led by the 3rd Armored Division in the south, and Ninth Army, led by the 2nd Armored in the north. The "Hell on Wheels" resumed its place as spearhead of the offensive.

CCB started off at 9:00 in the evening on March 29. After brief skirmishes at the Dortmund–Ems Canal, including a bridge blown literally in the faces of the 17th Engineers, a crossing was secured by morning. The next day a battalion each of the 67th Armored and 41st Armored Infantry ran into fanatic resistance from 200 German officer cadets. After 50 were killed by tank and mortar fire, 90 surrendered. At the next town, Ahlen, the entire population surrendered, some of the civilians cheering the American troops. Chaos erupted a short time later when a German train pulled in, not aware 2AD held the town. Both sides fumbled with their weapons until the 92nd AFA turned some of its guns around and blasted the train.

John Colliers' CCA followed up CCB by different routes to the canal and also met stiff resistance. Establishing a bridgehead by turning a barge sideways, advanced infantry soon silenced the defenders. CCA made 30 miles that day, at one point encountering opposition from Hitler Youth volunteers, some no more than 14 years old.

While stopping to have a meal at an inn in Ahlen, CCB's commander, Sidney Hinds, thought he'd place a phone call to the next town, Beckum, to warn it to surrender. The German commander got on the line and refused, so Hinds told him his tanks would be there at midnight and if one shot were fired, he'd level the town. Determined to follow up his threat, Hinds rushed CCB to Beckum, but it turned out the German troops had hastily evacuated.

Just after midnight on April 1, CCB received orders to head straight for Lippstadt at the tip of the rapidly forming

Below: Outside the Elbe-river city of Magdeburg on April 17, 1945. After the city refused to surrender to the 2nd Armored, Allied bombers levelled it, causing the tankers to be greeted with gruesome sights once they broke in. *U.S. Army via Real War Photos*

Ruhr pocket. Germans were still escaping from the encirclement and 2nd Armored needed to seal it in conjunction with 3rd Armored, which was racing up from the southern flank. When CCB arrived at Lippstadt it plunged into a desperate fight against thousands of Germans trying to break out. At 3:45 that afternoon, Easter Sunday, 2nd Armored linked with 3rd Armored to close the pocket. The latter had covered 90 miles in one day, a record for the ETO. Unfortunately, 3rd Armored's commander, Major General Maurice Rose, who had led "Hell on Wheels"' CCA in Normandy, was killed in action at Paderborn that night.

Infantry divisions soon lined the Ruhr pocket on both sides, forcing the surrender of 317,000 Germans. This gutted German resistance in the west, while 2nd Armored received orders to push onward to the east. CCA was already attacking through the Teutoburg Forest, where in the time of Caesar Augustus, three Roman legions had been destroyed by German tribesmen. The forest was both dense and hilly, and isolated German forces were still resisting. After entering the town of Oerlinghausen, a battalion of CCA was twice forced out by counterattacks. They finally flanked the enemy and cut off their rear, securing the town. While elements of the 30th Infantry Division moved up to clear out the woods, the 2nd Armored reached the Cologne–Berlin Autobahn, a modern highway, though wrecked bridges and overpasses hindered progress.

On April 4, Ninth Army reverted to U.S. command, and after consultations with Bradley, Simpson laid out his directives for the next stage of the advance. The 2nd Armored's initial objective would be the Elbe. Most of the tankers thought their ultimate objective was Berlin, unaware that Allied higher command had already decided to cede the German capital to the Russians.

That day, CCA arrived at the Weser River, where on April 5 it was joined by CCB on its right flank. All the bridges were blown but CCA engineers built one of their own, over which both combat commands crossed. As the division plowed deeper into Germany, it continued meeting the same phenomenon of some towns waving white flags and others still defended with fanatical defiance. And the threat of roving squads of diehards armed with Panzerfausts remained omnipresent. Some tankers had coated their vehicles with sandbags held together with nets, which helped to fend off the hollow-charge projectiles of these hand-held weapons.

After a pause for maintenance on April 8, CCA overran a German airfield with 83 planes. By now many Germans were surprised to see U.S. armored columns in their midst, often just rushing through towns before the Germans could even surrender. On the 10th, 2nd Armored began its final lunge to the Elbe. CCA ran into an industrial zone and for the first time since leaving the Rhine met concentrated artillery fire. It was from flak batteries protecting the Hermann Göring Steel Works, the gunners leveling their anti-aircraft 88s to fire at the tanks. CCB had an easier time on the right, advancing 20 miles.

Below: Another part of Krefeld on March 3, 1945, reflecting the previous day's fighting, as 2AD passes through on its way to the Rhine. *U.S. Army via Real War Photos*

On April 11, CCB began the day by shooting up a German truck convoy. Proceeding onward to Oschersleben, the 92nd AFA Battalion lost an SP gun to a Panzerfaust, but then 67th Armored tanks overran an airfield, finding 17 Me-109s on the ground. The Germans defended the airfield and during the firefight, the tankers shot down two enemy planes. A third was destroyed while trying to land by a round from a tank destroyer. After mopping up the airfield, the 67th Armored received calls for help from the 82nd Recon Battalion, which had not only run into heavy resistance but had run off its maps and was lost. The 1st Battalion/67th moved up and helped blast the way to the outskirts of the city of Magdeburg. On CCB's right, Col. Disney's column had proceeded without opposition for most of the day. At one point it caught up to an enemy marching column of 1,700 men, who all surrendered. After pausing for two hours, the column pressed further until at 8:00 in the evening it radioed 2nd Armored headquarters, "We're on the Elbe!" The "Hell on Wheels" had led all Allied divisions in the advance.

The tankers first reached the Elbe at Schönebeck, a town south of Magdeburg. German armor was retreating over a bridge and Major James Hollingsworth had the idea of following them discreetly in the dark with a tank company. His plan was foiled when Germans recognized the Shermans and the enemy opened up a torrent of fire from both sides of the river. The next morning the Germans blew the bridge.

The huge Russian attack on Berlin was still four days away, and the 2nd Armored encountered fierce German resistance to prevent its crossing the Elbe. The division opened talks to persuade the city of Magdeburg to surrender, but the mayor refused. CCA sealed off the city while CCB identified a bridging site to the south. Hinds had acquired 10 DUKWs and these ferried two battalions of 41st Armored Infantry and a battalion of the 30th Division's 119th Infantry to the far shore to hold a bridgehead. These men had no heavy weapons but it was thought that the 17th Engineers could quickly lay a pontoon bridge.

The Engineers began work after dark and by dawn on the 13th were halfway across the river when German artillery opened fire. Most of the pontoons were soon destroyed and the Engineers had to start over. 2nd Armored artillery units tried to silence the enemy guns, and smoke was placed in an attempt to conceal the crossing site. But the Germans only increased their fire. Three times the Engineers went back on the river to complete the bridge and each time lost more men and equipment. It was decided to shift the bridge farther south, out of range of the German guns. The three battalions on the east side were able to move to the south after dark and partially dig in. Early the next morning, however, the Germans counterattacked the bridgehead.

Hundreds of enemy troops backed by tanks and SP guns caved in 41st Armored Infantry's perimeter. The Americans had nothing but bazookas and machine guns to stop them. U.S. prisoners were used as

Below: Citizens of Berlin greet a tank of the 2nd Armored, the first U.S. division to enter the German capital in July 1945. *U.S. Army via Real War Photos*

human shields while Panzers simply fired into the foxholes. The two 41st battalions fell back on the infantry battalion in reserve closest to the river. 2AD artillery from the west side of the Elbe succeeded in halting any further German progress. Hinds received disturbing reports that one battalion might have been wiped out and that Col. Disney, commanding the bridgehead, was wounded. Hinds urgently requested air support but was told that none was available. The excuse was that the Allied offensive had outrun its tactical airfields, even though 2nd Armored had captured a number of intact airfields during its advance.

The Engineers' renewed effort to construct a bridge was defeated by German artillery fire, and in the early afternoon Hinds decided to abandon the bridgehead. By now there were only three remaining DUKWs, but these went back and forth ferrying the infantry while 2AD guns provided cover. By the time the withdrawal was completed, only one DUKW was still afloat. Some men swam the river, and 41st Armored Infantry survivors continued to arrive during the night.

Farther south at Barby, the 83rd Infantry Division had gotten across the Elbe with a completed bridge, and General White secured permission to pass part of CCB over. After the 2AD bridgehead had been lost, these troops helped defend the 83rd's positions until that bridgehead, too, was withdrawn.

Back at Magdeburg, the Germans were still refusing to surrender, and heavy bombers were called in to persuade them. James Provens, who had fought with 2AD since Normandy, thought the aftermath was the saddest event he witnessed in the war. When the 2nd Armored's CCA and the 30th Division finally entered the city they found hundreds of civilians blown apart by the air strike. Just weeks later, the war was over.

Unknown to Ninth Army's General Simpson, who had planned for the "Hell on Wheels" to spearhead his drive on Berlin, the Allied leadership had already decided to halt on the Elbe. Much to the dismay of the 2nd Armored, the death blow to Hitler's regime would be delivered by the Russians. During the attack from the Rhine to the Elbe, the 2nd Armored had lost 81 dead, 401 wounded and 153 missing. It had killed or wounded thousands of Germans and captured 45,022 prisoners. Though 2nd Armored's officers were disappointed at having to wait out the last few weeks of the war on the Elbe, they agreed with General Isaac White's assessment of his division in an order of the day: "No unit has written a brighter chapter in the history of the war."

Above: The Russians did not exactly welcome "Hell on Wheels" to Berlin in July 1945. Here engineers fix a bridge in order to open the route to the German capital. *U.S. Army via Real War Photos*

INSIGNIA, CLOTHING & EQUIPMENT

Opposite, above left: 2nd Armored shoulder patch and emblems of 66th and 67th Armored Regiments (above left and right), 41st Infantry ("Straight and Stalwart") and the 82nd Recon ("Audacia cum prudentia").

Opposite, above right: Sergeant "Ponzie" Ponczynski, of E Company, 41st Armored Infantry. Note the divisional patch on the left sleeve of his uniform jacket. *Courtesy of Mark Bando*

Opposite, below: Reenactors and an M4A1 Sherman. Note the armament: 75mm main gun, coaxial and hull-mounted .30 cal machine guns, and pintle-mounted M2HB .50 machine gun at the commander's station. *Tim Hawkins*

Below: Reenactor detail of the M1942 helmet. Note the spring that holds the earpieces in place, the goggles, and the 2nd Armored patch. *Tim Hawkins*

As an essentially standard division within the ranks of the U.S. Army, the 2nd Armored Division was very much clothed and equipped as other tank divisions — and as other soldiers within the U.S. Army. Clothing types evolved as new combat uniforms were introduced, but badges of rank and personal weapons were much the same as those of other units and remained as they had been before 1941. The U.S. Army pioneered the separation of combat and service dress, so in-theater soldiers wore few external signs of rank or unit identification (for obvious reasons), and a mixture of clothing would be found.

The main changes to the tank divisions during wartime were in the basic tools of their job: the armored vehicles, whether they were tanks, tank destroyers or armored cars. The 76mm-armed late-model M4 Shermans or M18 Hellcats, or 90mm M36 tank destroyers were a long way from the M3s and M4s that fought in the North African desert in 1942. This book is not going to examine the detail of these vehicle changes, but a photographic section at the end of this chapter provides a brief introduction to the subject.

The chapter starts by looking at the 2nd Armored's insignia and then gives some details on the distinctive combat clothing its men used, particularly in northwest Europe in 1944–45.

INSIGNIA

The divisional emblem (see artwork above right) was based on the standard emblem used by all U.S. armored divisions. The colors signify red for artillery, blue for infantry, and yellow for cavalry. The symbols represent the characteristics of armored divisions: the tank track, mobility and armor protection; the cannon, firepower; and the red bolt of lightning, shock action. What was slightly unusual about 2nd Armored's patch was that it was not just worn on the shoulder (see photos on pages 66 and 72) but also on the left breast ("over the heart") of some clothing. Patton started this to improve morale in the division (see photograph on page 84).

Each of the major units of 2nd Armored also had their emblems — some official, some unofficial — and examples are illustrated above right, such as those of the two tank regiments — the 66th Armored (the "Iron Knights") and the 67th. The 66th is the oldest armored unit in the U.S. Army, and can trace its lineage to the beginning of the Tank Service in February 1918. The regiment took part in the battle of St Mihiel, and in the Meuse-Argonne and the Somme offensives. The crest of the 66th makes use of the same colors and representations as the divisional emblem.

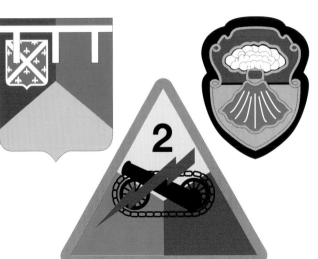

Right: Patton — while CG of 2nd Armored — poses in front of his M1A1 during the Louisiana Maneuvers of 1941. Note the flags of a two-star general and of the division. Patton wears tanker's green-grey coveralls. *Via George Forty*

Left: On the outskirts of Berlin in July 1945, a late model M4A3 passes a horse drawn supply cart of the Red Army, affording us a good view of the tank's markings and turret layout. With its 76mm gun (which necessitated a redesign of the turret), HVSS suspension and improved appliqué armour protection, this version of the Sherman was probably the best. Other improvements included "wet" stowage for the ammunition. This involved protecting the ammunition racks with glycerine. Some 1,500 M4A3s of this type were built by Detroit Arsenal, August–December 1944. *U.S. Army via Real War Photos*

Below left: A 67th Armored Regiment (note unit marking just visible on glacis) M4A3 passes a burned-out German halftrack on the side of a country road in Normandy during Operation Cobra. *U.S. Army via Chris Ellis*

Below: On the eve of Operation Cobra, members of the 2nd Battalion, 41st Armored Infantry pose in their new camouflage uniforms. These uniforms would soon be discarded because friendly formations would often mistake them for German SS or paratroopers. *Courtesy of Mark Bando*

Left: This reenactment photograph shows off the tanker's combat jacket, much prized by by non-tankers as well, on the man on the left. On his sleeve is the rank insignia of a technician grade 3. The man on the right wears a one-piece herringbone twill suit. Both wear the M1942 helmet. *Tim Hawkins*

Below left: Hand on the commander's 50-cal Browning, the man on the right wears a winter combat helmet. Both wear second-pattern HBT suits. Note the holstered 45. *Tim Hawkins*

Right and Below: The crew of the Sherman was five — commander (seen here), whose hatch was on the right side of the turret; gunner, whose position in the tank was almost immediately in front of the commander; loader/wireless operator (also known as the 'cannoneer'), whose hatch was on the left of the turret; driver, who sat on the left side of the transmission in the front of the hull; and assistant driver who sat front right and also manned the .30 cal hull-mounted machine gun. In these photographs the commander shows off the tanker's helmet and winter combat jacket. *Both: Tim Hawkins*

The roots of the 67th Armored Regiment go back to 1917, when 65th Engineer Battalion was a converted into a tank battalion and redesignated the 301st Tank Battalion (Heavy). After the Armistice it was banded together with the 303rd Tank Brigade under the command of General George S. Patton. In 1932 it became the medium tank regiment known as 67th Armored Regiment, the unit crest being an erupting volcano superimposed on a shield with a red top and a gold bottom.

CLOTHING

Tankers' Helmets

There were two types of helmet, neither of which was designed to offer ballistic protection — their main use was to protect heads from the unyielding metal and myriad sharp projections that make up the inside of a tank. Latterly, they housed radio earpieces. The first type lacked an integral radio headset and earpieces and was much disliked. The second, the M1942 composition helmet with a ventilated top, was much better (see photographs on page 71). The top was perforated leather with attached neck and cheek guards, the latter kept tight to the head by means of metal springs encased in leather. The helmet was painted olive green and had a tan leather lining that was visible at the edges of neck and cheek pieces. Another nice ergonomic touch was the way that the elastic straps of goggles could be attached to the helmet to ensure that they didn't become separated. Beneath the M1942 helmet tankers could wear the fabric helmet, part of the winter combat clothing (see below). To afford ballistic protection tankers (particularly among tank commanders when operating heads up or crews of open-topped vehicles such as tank destroyers) would wear the shell of the standard M1 helmet over the top of the helmet, although this proved too tight a fit for many.

HBT Overalls

One-piece grey-green HBT fatigue coveralls were introduced in 1942. There were two versions with minor differences (the first had breast pockets without buttons which were introduced on the second). They had an integral belt, no shoulder straps for rank badges, and were sometimes worn with leggings.

Winter Combat Clothing

In 1941 the first specialized tanker's uniform appeared — a weatherproofed cotton twill jacket with knitted wool cuffs (elasticated to ensure a tight fit), waistband, and collar, blanket lining and a zip front. Unlike most other combat clothing it had no straps at the shoulder for rank insignia. Early versions had patch pockets which were replaced by slash side pockets. From the end of 1943 there were also bib-fronted, blanket-lined cotton trousers that saw two main versions. The first had a zipper on the right side for access to pockets underneath and permanently attached suspenders. The second had access zippers on both sides, a zip fly (off center) and button and hook braces. Both had a full-length zip up the front from the crotch. Finally there was a fabric winter helmet liner that could be worn under a tanker's leather helmet (see photograph on page 75).

Camouflaged Uniform

Camouflaged uniforms started to appear in the U.S. Army in 1942, but it wasn't until June 1944 that they were issued to tankers (see photograph page 69). The uniform was two-piece and was extremely unpopular — particularly as its superficial similarity to the Waffen-SS camouflage clothing led to friendly fire problems in the Normandy bocage. Most soldiers changed back into the standard wool service shirt and trousers, or used tankers' coveralls or winter combat clothing instead.

Right: Halftrack driver Curtis O'Neill, of the 2nd Battalion, 41st Armored Infantry, takes a break on the German Westwall in October 1944. The concrete dragon's teeth funneled U.S. armor attacks into predictable routes covered by fire, unless engineers could blast holes through the emplacements. *Courtesy of Mark Bando*

Below: Jerry Kamarek of the division's 82nd Armored Reconnaissance Battalion. *Courtesy of Mark Bando*

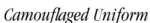

Left: Horse trading! This infantry sergeant (left) is after a tanker's combat jacket and is prepared to pay for it. The tanker wears bib-fronted trousers and has a 6th Armored flash on his sleeve above his staff sergeant's stripes. *Tim Hawkins*

Below, left and far left: Two more views of the bib-fronted winter combat trousers. *Tim Hawkins*

Right: The winter combat helmet is worn with 1944 Polaroid goggles. *Tim Hawkins*

ATTACHMENTS

Antiaircraft Artillery

195th AAA (AW) Bn (SP)	From 11 Jun 1944
Btys C & D, 129th AAA Gun Bn (Mbl)	25–30 Jul 1944
Btys A & B, 474th AAA (AW) Bn (SP)	28–31 Jul 1944

Armored

Sqn B, BR 1st Fife & Forfar Yeo (BR 79th Armd Div)	15–24 Nov 1944
40th Tk Bn (7th Armd Div)	23–24 Nov 1944
Sqn B, BR 1st Fife & Forfar Yeo (BR 79th Armd Div)	25 Dec 1944–18 Jan 1945
Elm, 738th Tk Bn (Mine Exploder)	12–17 Jan 1945
Co A, 739th Tk Bn	27 Feb–5 Mar 1945

Cavalry

24th Cav Recon Sqn	25–28 Jul 1944
113th Cav Recon Sqn	6–15 Aug 1944
1st Pl, 30th Recon Tp (30th Div)	7–12 Aug 1944
4th Cav Gp	23–31 Dec 1944

Engineer

Co B, 327th Engr C Bn (102nd Div)	16–25 Nov 1944
Co B, 105th Engr C Bn (30th Div)	2–16 Apr 1945

Field Artillery

65th Armd Fd Arty Bn	3–8 Jul 1944
65th Armd Fd Arty Bn	13 Jul–30 Sep 1944
62nd Armd Fd Arty Bn	25 Jul–22 Sep 1944
258th Fd Arty Bn (155mm Gun)	6–26 Aug 1944
258th Fd Arty Bn (155mm Gun)	3–30 Oct 1944
65th Armd Fd Arty Bn	5 Oct–21 Dec 1944
62nd Armd Fd Arty Bn	6–25 Oct 1944
70th Fd Arty Bn (105mm How)	25 Oct–3 Nov 1944
557th Fd Arty Bn (155mm Gun)	30 Oct–8 Nov 1944
83rd Armd Fd Arty Bn	4–24 Nov 1944
380th Fd Arty Bn (102nd Div) (105mm How)	17–25 Nov 1944
957th Fd Arty Bn (155mm How)	22 Dec 1944–17 Jan 1945
87th Armd Fd Arty Bn	22 Dec 1944–19 Jan 1945
65th Armd Fd Arty Bn	5 Feb–10 Mar 1945
696th Armd Fd Arty Bn	6 Feb–10 Mar 1945
258th Fd Arty Gp	26 Feb–5 Mar 1945
696th Armd Fd Arty Bn	26 Mar–19 Apr 1945
258th Fd Arty Bn (155 Gun)	26 Mar–19 Apr 1945
65th Armd Fd Arty Bn	27 Mar–19 Apr 1945
113th Fd Arty Bn (30th Div) (155mm How)	2–5 Apr 1945
197th Fd Arty Bn (30th Div) (105mm How)	2–17 Apr 1945

Infantry

22rd CT (4th Div)	21 Jul–1 Aug 1944
44th Fd Arty Bn (4th Div) (105mm How)	21 Jul–1 Aug 1944
1st Pl Co C, 4th Engr C Bn (4th Div)	21 Jul–1 Aug 1944
2nd Bn, 119th Inf (30th Div)	2–12 Aug 1944
3nd Bn, 119th Inf (30th Div)	3–4 Aug 1944
3nd Bn, 120th Inf (30th Div)	9–12 Aug 1944
3rd Bn, 8th Inf (4th Div)	11–14 Aug 1944
99th Inf Bn (Non-Div)	15 Aug–18 Sep 1944
3rd Bn, 116th Inf (29th Div)	4–29 Oct 1944
2nd Bn, 116th Inf (29th Div)	8–11 Oct 1944
405th Inf (102nd Div)	26 Oct–3 Nov 1944
1st Bn, 405th Inf (102nd Div)	3–6 Nov 1944
406th Inf (-1st Bn) (102nd Div)	6–25 Nov 1944
1st Bn, 406th Inf (102nd Div)	9–25 Nov 1944
2nd Bn, 119th Inf (30th Div)	11–28 Nov 1944
335th CT (84th Div)	22–24 Nov 1944
1st Bn, 119th Inf (30th Div)	25 Nov–3 Dec 1944
60th CT (9th Div)	22–23 Dec 1944
2nd Bn, 291st Inf (75th Div)	25–28 Dec 1944
1st, 2nd & 3rd Bns 335th Inf (84th Div)	1–10 Jan 1945
335th Inf (84th Div)	1–11 Jan 1945
1st & 2nd Bns 333d Inf (84th Div)	10–17 Jan 1945
3rd Bn, 333rd Inf (84th Div)	10–17 Jan 1945
331st Inf (83d Div)	28 Feb–1 Mar 1945
908th Fd Arty Bn (83d Div) (105 How)	28 Feb–1 Mar 1945
Co C, 308th Engr C Bn	28 Feb–1 Mar 1945
379th Inf (95th Div)	1–4 Mar 1945
377th Inf (95th Div)	29 Mar–2 Apr 1945
119th Inf (30th Div)	2–17 Apr 1945

Tank Destroyers

702nd TD Bn (SP)	11 Jun–21 Sep 1944
702nd TD Bn (SP)	1 Oct 1944–7 Feb 1945
Co A, 814th TD Bn (SP)	23–24 Nov 1944
702nd TD Bn (SP)	From 27 Feb 1945

Left: Two tankers, Medford and Ray, of F Company, 66th Armored Regiment, relax inside Germany in spring 1945. *Courtesy of Mark Bando*

Below: A 67th Armored Regiment tank on maneuvers in Georgia. The vehicle is an M2A4, armed with a 37mm main gun and three .30-cal machine guns. Used for training, it wouldn't see action in Europe. *Courtesy of Mark Bando*

Above: The 75mm T30 howitzer motor carriage was used by HQ companies of medium tank battalions until replaced by the M8 HMC in 1943. This one carries a 75mm M1A1 howitzer and is seen at Fort Benning in July 1942. *U.S. Army via Chris Ellis*

Left: The Gun Motor Carriages M10 (built on the M4A2 chassis) and M10A1 (built on the M4A3 chassis) equipped U.S. and British tank destroyer units. Over 6,000 were produced, around 1,000 being M10A1s which were mainly used for training or were converted into prime movers. In British service they were called Wolverines and from late 1944 many had the M7 3-inch gun replaced by 76mm OQF, being renamed Achilles. This M10 is seen outside Magdeburg on 17 April 1945 (see also pages 2/3). *U.S. Army via Real War Photos*

Far left: Crew of an M4A1 show off for the cameraman. *Tim Hawkins*

Above: Another successful design, the M18 Hellcat tank destroyer, was armed with a 76mm gun and had a crew of five (commander, driver, three gunners). Over 2,500 were built before production ceased in October 1944. Hellcats equipped TD battalions in Italy and northern Europe, where their firepower and speed made them effective performers.
U.S. Army via George Forty

Above right: The M36 GMC was an improved version of the M10 with a 90mm M3 in place of the M7 three-inch gun of the M10. This led to a new turret design but the same crew of five (commander, driver, three gunners). Introduced in late 1944 they proved very successful, providing U.S. armored divisions with an effective counter to the German heavy tanks.
U.S. Army via George Forty

Right: The M26 Pershing heavy tank first saw service with U.S. 3rd and 9th Armored Divisions in NW Europe in January 1945, too late to have been of use during the devastating armored battles of 1944. Nevertheless, full production was ordered immediately and the Pershing saw action in the Pacific during the battle for Okinawa and would continue in service into the Korean War. This photograph shows 2nd Armored Pershings in Magdeburg. *U.S. Army via George Forty*

Far right: The M5 light was a development of the earlier M3 with twin Cadillac engines. These necessitated modifications to the vehicle — particularly to the rear engine covers. Sporting a 37mm main weapon, M3s and M5 Stuarts — called the Honey in British service — saw use as reconnaissance vehicles until superseded by the M24 Chaffee. *U.S. Army via George Forty*

ENEMY UNITS ENCOUNTERED BY THE DIVISION JUNE 13, 1944–JANUARY 1945

Unit	Location	Date	Unit	Location	Date
17th SS Pz Div	Carentan	June 13	277th Inf Div (elem)	Elbeuf	Aug 26–27
6th FJ Regt	Carentan	June 13	18th Luftwaffe Div	Elbeuf	Aug 29–30
2nd Pz Div	Caumont	June 23	33rd Luftwaffe Regt	Elbeuf	Aug 29–30
275th Inf Div	Caumont area	June 23	49th Inf Div (elem)	Beauvais	Aug 31
3rd FJ Div (elem)	Caumont area	June 23	85th Inf Div (elem)	Tournai, Belgium	Sept 2
2nd SS Pz Div	South of St Lô	July 13–14	47th Inf Div (elem)	St. Trond-Tongres	Sept 8
Panzer Lehr Div	St Lô breakthrough	July 26–27	SS Div *Nederland*	Hasselt	Sept 8
5th FJ Div	St Lô breakthrough	July 27–28	16th Security Regt	Hasselt	Sept 12
353th Inf Div	Vire and west of Vire	July 28	176th Div	Hasselt	Sept 13
243th Inf Div	Cerisy-la-Salle	July 29	22nd Luftwaffe Regt	Hasselt	Sept 17
363th Inf Div	Fôret de St. Seves	Aug 4	183rd Volks Gren Div	Geilenkirchen, Germ'y	Sept 24
84th Inf Div	Barenton	Aug 8	54th Fortress MG Bn	Alsdorf	Oct 2
116th Pz Div	Mortain	Aug 9	33rd Fortress MG Bn	Alsdorf	Oct 2
277th Inf Div	Mortain-Barenton	Aug 9	42nd Fortress MG Bn	Alsdorf	Oct 5
10th SS Pz Div	Mortain-Barenton	Aug 10	246th Volks Gren Div	S of Geilenkirchen	Oct 6
91st Inf Div (elem)	Barenton	Aug 14	NCOs School *Julich*	Geilenkirchen	Oct 11
1st SS Pz Div (elem)	Falaise Pocket	Aug 15	NCOs School *Duren*	Geilenkirchen	Oct 11
352nd Inf Div (elem)	Falaise Pocket	Aug 16	9th Pz Div	Gereonsweiler	Dec 4–10
17th Construction Bn	Domfront	Aug 16	15th Pz Gren Div	Gereonsweiler	Dec 4–10
158th Construction Bn	Domfront	Aug 16	10th SS Pz Div	Gereonsweiler	Dec 4–10
344th Inf Div	Damville	Aug 22	340th Volks Gren Div	Julich	Dec 4–10
17th Luftwaffe Div	Damville	Aug 22	2nd Pz Div	Celles, Belgium	Dec 25
271st Inf Div (elem)	Elbeuf	Aug 26–27	560th Volks Gren Div	Marche-Hotton	Jan 1945

Right: Know your enemy! German armor designers learned the early war lessons well. The 75mm-armed PzKpfw V Panther and 88mm-armed PzKpfw VI Tiger (seen here) proved far superior to Allied tanks during the war. In the end, attrition and the sheer number of Allied vehicles defeated the "zoo" beasts. A good, if much-quoted, example of the mismatch is shown by the fight near Villers-Bocage on June 13, 1944, where Tigers of the 501st Heavy Tank Battalion destroyed a column of British vehicles, one of the Panzer VI commanders, Obersturmführer Michael Wittmann, personally accounting for 25 vehicles, including 12 tanks. *Via Chris Ellis*

Above: M4 medium in Tunisia. Having first seen action at El Alamein in October 1942, the Sherman became the workhorse of Allied armored units in every theater of World War II. By the time of Operation Torch it was the 2nd Armored's primary medium tank, alongside the M5 Stuart light.
U.S. Army via Chris Ellis

Left: Another late model M4A3 (see also page 68 top photo) with 76mm gun and HVSS suspension. This one — *Elsie* — in the streets of shattered Berlin has attracted a group of children in July 1945. The generosity of U.S. troops had quickly become famous among the devastated civilians of Europe.
U.S. Army via Real War Photos

PEOPLE

General George Patton (1885–1945)

Patton was not only one of the most colorful figures in the 2nd Armored but in all of U.S. military history. Born to a wealthy California family with a long military heritage from Virginia, he graduated from West Point in 1909 as a 2nd Lieutenant of Cavalry. He participated in General John Pershing's pursuit of Pancho Villa in Mexico, and then served on Pershing's staff when the AEF went to France to join in the Great War. Unsatisfied with staff work, Patton formed and trained the fledgling U.S. Tank Corps, and led it in battle at St. Mihiel and the Meuse-Argonne (where he was wounded).

Between the wars Patton returned to the horse cavalry, but with the new war looming and the 2nd Armored Division activated in July 1940, he arrived to command its 1st Brigade. Ten weeks later he took over the division. Patton's leadership of the 2nd Armored — his only divisional command — helped place the Hell on Wheels in first place among U.S. combat formations. After Pearl Harbor he was promoted to command I Armored Corps, and then led the Western Task Force in Operation Torch, with 2nd Armored under his command. He briefly took over II Corps, before returning to I Corps to prepare the invasion of Sicily. Off the Sicilian coast, this force was renamed Seventh Army, Patton as commander. Competing with British Eighth Army, Patton arranged for the seizure of Palermo, Sicily's capital and largest city, and then beat the British to Messina, doing much to erase the perception that the Americans were inferior to the British. But during the Sicilian campaign, Patton got into deep trouble by slapping two soldiers suffering from nervous exhaustion. The incidents caused an outcry and he was forced to apologize at assemblies of all U.S. divisions in Sicily. He chose the 2nd Armored as his first audience, and the men received him with polite disinterest. (The 1st Infantry were more rude.) The upshot was that Mark Clark and Omar Bradley leapt above Patton in the U.S. command structure.

The Germans still held a high regard for Patton, and in the run-up to the Normandy invasion he was named head of a "phantom" army in southeast England, on the theory that the Germans couldn't possibly believe that Bradley would lead the main U.S. thrust. Patton's Third Army was activated for real on August 1, 1944, after the 2nd Armored had played the lead role in forcing a gap in the Normandy front. This allowed Patton to gain his perfect milieu, combining dashing cavalry tactics with heavy firepower in the interior of France, and pure boldness in either case. When the war was over, Patton reviewed the 2nd Armored, which had been designated the first U.S. division to enter Berlin. It is said that he never lost affection for the "Hell on Wheels", and he nostalgically told some of its officers that if it had remained under his command, "We really could have gone to town." Though the 2nd Armored had done well enough on its own during the war, that sense of pride was reciprocated. The following December Patton was killed near Mannheim, Germany in a traffic accident.

Major General Ernest N. Harmon (1894–1979)

After Patton, "Ol' Gravel Voice" was the most famous commander of the 2nd Armored. Graduating from West Point in 1917 as a 1st Lieutenant of Cavalry, he took part in the

Below: The best U.S. general of the war? Probably. Patton is dressed in a Parsons field jacket and a helmet liner. On his left breast — the location he proposed for morale reasons — is the 2nd Armored patch.
via George Forty

St. Mihiel and Meuse-Argonne battles in which America's Tank Corps debuted. When the 2nd Armored was activated in July 1940 he was chief of staff of Armored Force headquarters, and was given the division in July 1942. After leading the division (and one of the invasion sub-task forces) in Morocco, he was dispatched to Tunisia to retrieve the chaos caused by Rommel's Kasserine offensive. Harmon arrived hours after Rommel had decided to withdraw; nevertheless, his sure-handed direction solidifed the front and renewed U.S. confidence. In the process, Harmon made a poor assessment of II Corps commander Lloyd Fredendall. He was offered command of the corps but declined because he felt it was incorrect to assume the post of an officer he had personally criticized. After a brief return to the 2nd Armored, Harmon was called to take over the 1st Armored in April 1943. He subsequently led "Old Ironsides" at Salerno and Anzio and the conquest of Rome. In September 1944 Harmon was promoted to command a new corps forming up in Texas, but U.S. Chief of Staff George Marshall told him that command of the 2nd Armored had opened up with the similar promotion of Edward Brooks. Harmon returned to the division in September 12, 1944, just in time for the toughest battles of the war, against the Westwall, the Roer, and in the Ardennes.

Above: "Ol' Gravel Voice," Major General Ernest N. Harmon.

Among Harmon's many stellar achievements as an energetic (and relentlessly profane) commander, his destruction of the German spearhead in the Battle of the Bulge stands foremost. Though encouraged by Montgomery to remain on the defensive, Harmon, in collaboration with VII Corps' "Lightning Joe" Collins, decided to attack. The spearhead of the 2nd Panzer Division was soon obliterated, and follow-up German divisions reeled back from the Meuse. Harmon's aggressive instincts preserved the credit for winning the battle in U.S. hands. Montgomery had arrayed his powerful XXX Corps on the west side of the Meuse; Harmon made sure the Germans never even got to the river. After the Battle of the Bulge, Harmon finally agreed to command a corps, which performed occupation duty after VE-Day. He resigned from the Army in 1948 at age 54 and became president of Norwich University until 1965. Splitting his retirement years between Florida and Vermont, he died in 1979.

Major General Isaac D. White (1901–1990)

An early pioneer in armored forces, White became a 1st Lieutenant in the 1st Cavalry Regiment (Mechanized) in 1933. At 2nd Armored's inception he was a major commanding its 2nd (later 82nd) Recon Battalion. A colonel by the time of the N. African campaign, he led CCB in Sicily and then, as a brigadier general, in Normandy. His combat command's exploit in Operation Cobra, where it set an example that should have been imitated at Argentan-Falaise, is one of the great stories of U.S. combat heroism. White took command of the 2nd Armored after the Battle of the Bulge and led it through the rest of the war, leaving in June 1945 to become head of the Cavalry School at Fort Riley, Kansas. Today the main entrance to Norwich University in Connecticut is called General I.D. White Avenue.

Major General Hugh J. Gaffey (1895–1946)

A specialist in both artillery and armor, Gaffey was a Lt. Colonel at the time of 2AD's activation and commanded CCB in Morocco. After that brief bout against the French, he became chief of staff under Patton in II Corps, and then commander of 2nd Armored on May 5, 1943 after Harmon went to the 1st Armored. Gaffey led 2nd Armored through Sicily and the occupation that followed, but was reluctantly pulled from the division in March 1944 when Patton began to form his Third Army. Gaffey served as Third Army's chief of staff until early December when he became commander of the 4th Armored, going on to lead that division in its famous drive to Bastogne. He died in 1946 in the crash of a B-25 bomber and afterward a 17,000-ton transport ship was named the *General Hugh J. Gaffey* in his honor. Coincidentally, the ship was sunk in a live-fire exercise on June 16, 2000, the 54th anniversary of the General's death.

Above: Major General William D. Crittenberger, who succeeded George Patton as commander of the 2nd Armored Division, in the turret of his command tank at Fort Benning. The two-star flag designates the tank, an M3 light, as the commanding general's; at the top is the flag of the division. *via Chris Ellis*

Below right: Sgt. Hulon B. Whittington, 41st Armored Infantry, won two ADs and the division's first Medal of Honor, the latter during Operation Cobra in July 1945. *U.S. Army*

INDIVIDUAL AWARDS

CMH	2
DCS	21
Legion of Merit	13
Silver Star	1,954
Soldiers Medal	131
Bronze Star	5,331
Air Medal	342

Major General Maurice Rose (1899–1945)

Rose joined the army as a buck private in 1916, and by 1942, as a colonel, was chief of staff of the 2nd Armored. He went with Harmon to solve the problems in Tunisia after Kasserine, but returned to the division in May 1943 to lead CCA in Sicily. In Normandy, Rose was leading CCA in the vicious slugging match outside Vire, France when he was tapped to take over the 3rd Armored Division. He went on to lead the 3rd through the Bulge and beyond, earning personal honors of a DSM, Silver Star with two Oak Leaf Clusters, and many other awards. Rose was killed on March 30, 1945, at Paderborn, Germany, just as the 3rd Armored was joining hands with the 2nd Armored to close the Ruhr Pocket. His command convoy was ambushed by German infantry after dark and while trying to escape, Rose's jeep was suddenly faced by a Panther. The enemy tank commander ordered them to surrender. It is unclear whether Rose reached for his sidearm; in any event the German killed him with his machine pistol. Rose had several good reasons not to be taken prisoner. First, he was the CG of a U.S. armored division; second, he was Jewish; and third, he had commanded "Hell on Wheels" CCA at Carentan in June 1944, when the Germans had dubbed the division "Roosevelt's Butchers." He could not have expected an easy time in captivity.

Major General Edward H. Brooks (1893–1978)

Along with Harmon, Brooks was the only 2nd Armored commander in WWII to come from outside the division. An artilleryman, he fought with the 3rd "Rock of the Marne" Division in WWI, and early in WWII he helped to develop the M8 assault gun (75mm), used principally by the armored infantry, and the M7 SP gun (105mm) that proved a mainstay to Armored Field Artillery battalions. Brooks took command of the 2nd Armored in the spring before D-Day and led it through Normandy and the pursuit across France, Belgium, and Holland that followed. He left the division during the pause before the Westwall, on September 12, 1944, when he was promoted to command VI Corps. In 1947 he became commander of Third Army, and during the Korean War served in the office of the U.S. Chief of Staff.

Brigadier General Sidney R. Hinds (1900–1991)

Raised in North Dakota, Hinds graduated from West Point in 1920 and was assigned as a major to the 41st Armored Infantry at the division's inception. Taking over the 2nd Battalion in 1941, he was promoted full colonel in command of the regiment in 1942. After fighting at the forefront of the advance in Sicily, he fought another battle in England against General Hugh Gaffey, who wanted to put armored infantry in trucks. Hinds maintained that they were a special breed for whom halftracks were essential. He won the point (and also may have been influential in the argument to keep 2nd Armored a "heavy" armored division).

After "Hell on Wheels" had pried open the door to France for Patton's army, the neophyte 4th Armored Division mistakenly fired its first shots of the campaign at the 2nd Armored. Hinds got on the radio and told them to stop or else he would tell their "P," meaning General John P. (for "Professor") Wood. It was Hinds, with Brig. Gen. John Collier, who demanded a receipt from the British for the town of Elbeuf on the Seine, just before Hinds was ripped by Nebelwerfer fire (but refused to be evacuated).

His greatest exploit took place the following March when he all but seized an intact bridge over the Rhine, a week before Remagen. Finding no cooperation at 21st Army Group, and perhaps little from his accompanying infantry, Hinds sent two volunteer patrols across and back, proving the bridge could have been taken at a rush. The entire course of the war might have been altered if Hinds had received support. Promoted to Brig. General and command of CCB in 1945, his enthusiasm for the offensive again outpacing that of the Allied leadership when he established a short-lived bridgehead across the Elbe in April (which was refused air support). After WWII and before Korea, Hinds designed the Town & Country air rifle, based on the M1, which became the standard training rifle for the ASA.

Sgt. Hulon B. Whittington (1921–1969)

Whittington won 2nd Armored's first Medal of Honor on the night of July 29/30 during Operation Cobra. At the time, a column of at least 90 German vehicles and 2,500 personnel were trying to crash through CCB's thin line to rejoin the German front at Percy. Whittington, a squad leader in the 41st Armored Infantry, assumed command of his platoon when his lieutenant and the platoon sergeant went missing. He reorganized the defense and, under fire, courageously crawled between gun positions to check the actions of his men. When the enemy attempted to penetrate a roadblock, Sgt. Whittington mounted a tank and by shouting through the turret, directed it into position to fire pointblank at the leading German armored vehicle. Its destruction blocked all movement of the enemy column. The blocked vehicles were then destroyed by hand grenades, bazookas, tank, and artillery fire and large numbers of enemy personnel were wiped out by a bold and resolute bayonet charge. When the medical aid man became a casualty, Whittington personally administered first aid to his wounded men. His official citation read, "The dynamic leadership, the inspiring example, and the dauntless courage of Whittington above and beyond the call of duty, are in keeping with the highest traditions of the military service." He remained in the Army, went to Vietnam in a training capacity, before retiring in 1967. Sadly, in January 1969, he committed suicide with a .45.

Captain James F. Burt (1917–   )

During the final offensive against Aachen, on October 13, 1944, Captain James Burt won the Medal of Honor while in command of B Co. of the 66th Armored Regiment. As his official citation reads, "In the first day's action, when infantrymen ran into murderous small-arms and mortar fire, Captain Burt dismounted from his tank about 200 yards to the rear and moved forward on foot beyond the infantry positions, where . . . he calmly motioned his tanks into good firing positions. As the ground attack gained momentum, he climbed aboard his tank and directed the action from the rear deck, exposed to hostile volleys which finally wounded him painfully in the face and neck. He maintained his dangerous post despite pointblank gunfire until friendly artillery knocked out the enemy weapons, and then proceeded to the advanced infantry scout's position to deploy his tanks for the defense of the gains which had been made.

"The next day, when the enemy counterattacked, he went to assist the infantry battalion commander who was seriously wounded. For the next eight days . . . Captain Burt held the combined forces together, dominating and controlling the critical situation . . . To direct artillery fire, on October 15, he took his tank 300 yards into the enemy lines where he remained for an hour giving accurate data to friendly gunners. Twice more that day he went into enemy territory under deadly fire on reconnaissance. In succeeding days . . . twice the tank in which he was riding was knocked out and each time he climbed aboard another vehicle and continued to fight. He took great risks to rescue wounded comrades and inflicted prodigious destruction on enemy personnel and material, even though suffering from his own wounds. Captain Burt's intrepidity and disregard of personal safety was so complete that his own men and the infantry who attached themselves to him were inspired to overcome the wretched and extremely hazardous conditions which accompanied one of the most bitter local actions of the war. The victory achieved closed the Aachen gap."

A better description could not be written of the intensity of the often-neglected battles on the Westwall in fall 1944, including the heroism shown by the combat leaders of 2AD. James Burt returned to civilian life after the war, and after a career in the newspaper production business, is now enjoying retirement with his wife in Wyomissing, Pennsylvania.

2nd ARMORED SENIOR PERSONNEL

Commanding Officers
Maj. Gen Charles L. Scott - Jul 1940
Maj. Gen George S. Patton, Jr. - Jan 1941
Maj. Gen Willis D. Crittenberger - Feb 1942
Maj. Gen Ernest N. Harmon - Jul 1942
Maj. Gen Hugh J. Gaffey - May 1943
Maj. Gen Edward H. Brooks - April 1944
Maj. Gen Ernest N. Harmon - Sept 1944
Maj. Gen Isaac D. White - Jan 1945
Brig. Gen John H. Collier - May 1945
Maj. Gen John M. Devine - Aug 1945

Artillery Commander
Col. Thomas A. Roberts Jr -24 Nov 1943
Lt. Col. Carl I. Hutton -5 Aug 1944
Col. Carl I. Hutton -2 Nov 1944

Chiefs of Staff
Col. Redding F. Perry -24 Nov 1943
Col. Charles D. Parner -18 Mar 1944
Col. Clayton J. Mansfield -29 Sep 1944
Col. Gustavus W. West -30 Dec 1944

CCA Commander
Brig. Gen. Rose -24 Nov 1943
Col. John H. Collier -4 Aug 1944
Brig. Gen. John H. Collier -12 Nov 1944

CCB Commander
Col. Isaac D. White -24 Nov 1943
Brig. Gen. Isaac D. White -28 May 1944
Col. Sidney R. Hinds -19 Jan 1945
Brig. Gen. Sidney R. Hinds -21 Mar 1945

POSTWAR

Above: U.S. Chief of Staff George C. Marshall inspects the "Hell on Wheels" in Berlin on July 18, 1945. *U.S. Army via Real War Photos*

After V-E Day on May 8, 1945, the 2nd Armored assumed occupation duties in northern Germany. On the day after Hitler's suicide on April 30, the Germans discontinued organized resistance in the West and instead focused on escaping there. Hundreds of thousands of Wehrmacht troops, mixed with civilians, poured across the Elbe into Ninth Army's sector, an even greater number trekking into British lines to the north at Lübeck. Amidst this sea of retreaters and refugees, freed prisoners and concentration camp survivors, and a dismantled government apparatus in which former Nazis were no longer allowed, the 2nd Armored improvised. While providing security for the area, it appointed the most competent civilians available to keep order and organize the clean-up of rubble, just as Patton was doing farther south. In some cases this meant turning a blind eye while burghers discarded their armbands and continued their previous roles.

The postwar arrangement called for Russian occupation of eastern Germany; however, Berlin, in the Russian zone, was to be divided between the four conquering Allied powers. As the passions of war faded, the United States determined to make a show of strength in Berlin. Tensions with the Soviet Union had already risen due to its placing of Communist regimes in power in Poland, Hungary, Romania and elsewhere. Churchill had warned America about Russian designs all along, and now that FDR had been replaced by Truman the U.S. began to take heed. From over 100 divisions in the ETO, it was decided to send the 2nd Armored into Berlin as America's best foot forward.

The "Hell on Wheels" began its march to Berlin on July 1, 1945, only to find the Soviets had provided weak bridges, prohibitive to armor. A quick detour and the expertise of the 17th Engineer Battalion solved the problem, and on the 4th of July the 2nd Armored entered the German capital. The troops were surrounded by signs of devastation, as well as by crowds of German kids and civilians. After two years of bombing, the final Götterdämmerung on the ground, and then two months of Russian occupation, one can only imagine the relief of Berliners when the American 2nd Armored rolled into their city. West Berlin, consisting of the three non-Soviet zones, thence became an island of democracy behind the Iron Curtain for almost half a century.

On July 17, the Potsdam Conference began, involving Truman, Churchill (replaced midway by Clement Atlee), and Josef Stalin, with the 2nd Armored providing an honor guard. A few days later U.S. Secretary of War Harry Stimson, Chief of Staff George Marshall and General George Patton reviewed the full "Hell on Wheels". Patton never seemed to have lost his deep pride in the only division he had personally led. Despite his worries about Russian intentions, "The review was great," he wrote to his wife. On August 9 the 2AD resumed its occupation duties in West Germany. As one of the first divisions to arrive in the ETO it had a lot of high "point" men who had gone home after the surrender. In late December 1945, the entire division departed from Europe at Calais.

During the Cold War the 2nd Armored, based at Fort Hood, Texas, stood ready to resist any Soviet aggressions in Europe. It was mobilized in 1948 when the Russians tried to strangle the Western zones of Berlin, a crisis that was solved by a massive Anglo-American airlift. During the Cuban Missile Crisis of 1962 it was again put on alert, and some units began moving to Florida. During the Korean War, an offshoot of the 66th Armored Regiment, the 6th Battalion, saw action against the Communists, winning seven Battle Streamers and a Presidential Unit Citation.

Korea, like Vietnam, was a poor environment for armored divisions and the division spent most of its overseas time in Germany. During the 1970s the army — then in a cost-cutting spiral — began a series of six-month rotations so that troops would not have to bring dependents. Commanders of the 2nd Armored likewise rotated quickly during the Cold War, the division viewed as a prestigious stepping stone for further promotion. In August 1975 a nice bit of symmetry occurred when George S. Patton, Jr., took over the division.

In 1989 the Soviet Union began to collapse, with the effect that dictators around the world were no longer frozen by the Cold War but could now act on their own without fear of nuclear holocaust. In August 1990, Iraq's Saddam Hussein launched an unprovoked attack against his neighbor, Kuwait, occupying that country with heavy armored forces. In the interim the U.S. Army had switched from a combat command to a brigade system, and the 2nd Armored's 1st "Tiger" Brigade shipped to the Persian Gulf to counterattack. In February 1991 the 2nd Armored, flanked by Marine regiments, attacked the boundary of the Iraqi III and IV Corps, overrunning three entrenched infantry brigades and destroying or chasing two Iraqi armored divisions. After 100 hours of battle the tally for the 1st Brigade was 181 destroyed or captured enemy tanks, 148 APCs, 40 artillery pieces, 27 AA emplacements, 263 Iraqi dead and 4,051 captured. 2nd Armored's losses were two dead and five wounded. While the "Hell on Wheels" had once struggled against superior foreign tanks on the battlefield, by 1991 the U.S. Abrams tank and Bradley IFVs had proved markedly superior to any armor the Soviets or their clients could design.

After the demise of Communism and the crushing defeat delivered to Iraq, U.S. Army troops levels, which had averaged two million during the Cold War, shrunk drastically to around 500,000. The evolution of technology also took a hand in shifting force levels. An independent armored force, once so urgent after the German Blitzkrieg, had been rendered obsolete by the fact that all U.S. divisions were now armored and motorized. The need to spearhead infantry with elite armored formations no longer existed.

In December 1995 — in the center of the longest run of peace and prosperity the U.S. has ever enjoyed — the 2nd Armored Division was deactivated. Its 41st Armored Infantry Regiment went to the 1st Armored Division, based at the old cavalry post, Fort Riley. To the chagrin of many vets, the 1st Armored now calls itself the "oldest and most prestigious" armored division in the U.S. Army. As for the unit that truly holds the lineage of the oldest armored unit in the Army — direct descendants of the U.S. Tank Corps in World War I — 2nd Armored's 66th Armored and its sister regiment the 67th are now part of the 4th Infantry Division (Mechanized), based at Fort Hood. The 4th Division's 1st Brigade contains the 1st and 3rd Battalions of the 66th's "Iron Knights"; its 2nd Brigade has the 1st and 3rd Battalions of the 67th Regiment. The Abrams M1A1 tank remains the weapon-of-choice for U.S. armored units, though the 3rd/67th is equipped with a variation, the M1A2.

Army reorganization and nomenclature would be of purely academic interest, except that at this writing the 4th Infantry was in transit to the Mideast for a renewal of the Gulf War. The division was intended to open a northern front against Baghdad, in conjunction with the 3rd Infantry Division and Marine and British expeditionary forces attacking from the south. With the southern drive stalled after ten days of battle, 4th Infantry's equipment was rerouted through the Suez Canal to the Persian Gulf while its men flew across the Atlantic from Fort Hood. Possessing the skills and legacy of the "Hell on Wheels", the 4th Infantry had a profound impact on the final battle against Saddam Hussein.

Below: Another view of the Berlin parade on July 18, 1945. Note the Company E 66th Armored Regiment guidon. The white blob is the silhouette of a World War I British Mark V tank. Note, too, the fact that in peace the tankers' usual combat clothing has been replaced by wool service jackets and M1 helmets.
U.S. Army via Real War Photos

ASSESSMENT

Above: In May 1945, after VE-Day, the 2nd Armored Division marked its bivouac with a sign summarizing its achievements in the ETO.
Courtesy of Mark Bando

The 2nd Armored finished World War II among the first rank of U.S. combat formations. As one of America's seminal armored divisions (along with the 1st) and one of only two "heavy" armored divisions in northern Europe (the other was the 3rd), the 2nd Armored Division was a queen on the chessboard of U.S. military planners from North Africa to the occupation of Berlin. The division fought through many of the most terrific battles in U.S. history; yet somehow the "Hell on Wheels" has fallen outside the sightlines of many American histories of the war.

The explanations are several, and have nothing to do with the excellent combat record of the division. Ironically, the only time the 2nd Armored grabbed U.S. headlines was when Patton assigned it to seize Palermo, Sicily in July 1943. It was a weakly opposed advance, in the opposite direction from German strength on the island; yet it gained enormous press recognition. In subsequent campaigns the "Hell on Wheels" would stay at grips with the enemy, in relative obscurity, while Patton earned his headlines with other divisions.

During the Normandy campaign, the public temporarily became depressed by the seemingly interminable slugging match in summer 1944. It only became exhilarated when Patton's Third Army broke out into France, taking town after town, exceeding even the speed of the German breakthrough in 1940. The fact that 2nd Armored and the rest of First Army were still fighting it out with elite German divisions, advancing yard by yard against ferocious opposition, was less exciting. While Third Army measured its gains in miles, to paraphrase Bradley, 2nd Armored measured its gains in enemy dead. But the public, then and since, has preferred the spectacle of unopposed gains to close-quarters struggles against enemy strength.

It is probably a misfortune for the 2nd Armored that its hardest battles of the war took place in a small area north of Aachen, between the Wurm and Roer Rivers, in the soggy, gray autumn of 1944. The place-names involved, such as Ubach, Puffendorf, Apweiler or Geilenkirchen, mean little to casual students of the war; yet on that stretch of the German Westwall, soaked with both blood and freezing rain, the 2nd Armored fought its most difficult battles against the Wehrmacht. The "Hell on Wheels" finally prevailed, helping to drive a bulge into Germany, but this soon became forgotten as the Germans forced a greater indentation into the Allied front in the Ardennes.

In the Battle of the Bulge, the 2nd Armored smashed the German spearhead on Christmas Day (prior to the relief of Bastogne) but one can look in vain for a reference to this action in many accounts of the battle. In this case, 2nd Armored's enforced obscurity brings us to inter-Allied politics, or purposeful deception. By all rights, kudos in that battle should have gone to the division that obliterated the most advanced elements of the German offensive. After all, that was the point. The "Hell on Wheels" swept in from the north and crushed its counterpart, 2nd Panzer, just short of the Meuse. It further pushed back Panzer Lehr, the fresh 9th Panzer, and all other units which had bypassed

Bastogne to rush for the river. Hitler's strategic goal to cross the Meuse for an advance on Liége and Antwerp was thwarted by the U.S. 2nd Armored, and the attempt was not to be renewed.

The problem is that an enduring embarrassment to the United States has been Eisenhower's decision, on December 19, 1944, to place all U.S. forces to the north of the Bulge under British Field Marshal Montgomery's command. The German offensive had been launched straight into the center of Omar Bradley's U.S. 12th Army Group, yet when the U.S. faced its first great challenge in the ETO, Bradley was stripped of two-thirds of his command. He was left only with Patton's Third Army in the south while the U.S. First and Ninth Armies fell to British control. Montgomery aggravated the situation by stating that the Americans had suffered "a proper defeat," and then implied that he had personally solved the problem. The result was that at the time, and ever since, Americans have focused on Bastogne as the key to the battle. It was there that the 101st Airborne Division said "Nuts" to a German offer to surrender, and there that Patton's 4th Armored Division eventually rescued the gallant paratroopers to enduring acclaim.

2nd Armored's decisive obliteration of the German spearhead was all but covered up at the time by the spinmeisters at 12th Army Group and has been largely forgotten since. To Bradley and Patton, Bastogne had to be the key to the battle as it was presented to the U.S. public. (Indeed, once "Hell on Wheels" had crushed his spearhead, Hitler cooperated by focusing on that city.) Those U.S. divisions controlled by Monty on the northern flank were doomed to neglect despite their blunting the true aim of the offensive and their incurring heavier casualties. Ironically, the 2nd Armored Division had launched its Christmas attack on the German spearhead contrary to Montgomery's advice — Ernest Harmon and Joe Collins taking matters into their own hands. But U.S. initiative in the north could not surmount U.S. PR in the south, as long as the joint headquarters of Bradley and Patton had anything to say about it. In subsequent works on the battle, 7th Armored's brave stand near St. Vith has seen the light of day, but seldom has it been noted that 2nd Armored, as well as 3rd Armored, suffered more killed and wounded during the battle.

When 2nd Armored subsequently became the first division to fight its way through brutal enemy fire and just as terrible weather to Houffalize, thereby cutting the Bulge in half, this achievement, too, was diminished because it had been Monty's idea. The 2nd Armored lost 1,200 men and equal non-battle casualties to achieve an objective that the U.S. high command later disparaged. Bradley's subsequent "Hurry Up" offensive collapsed in the winter snows that "Hell on Wheels" had surmounted.

Since 2nd Armored returned to Ninth Army after the Bulge, still under British command, it was unfortunately placed in a position where U.S. XII Army Group was loath to acknowledge it, and at the same time the British wanted to relegate it to a subsidiary role in their massive operation to cross the Rhine. The only positive development for the division was that Simpson's Ninth Army turned out to be a crack outfit. As soon as the British provided bridge space, the "Hell on Wheels" charged into Germany, outpacing its neighbors. Once the 2nd Armored had joined hands with its old friend the 3rd (led by 2nd Armored alumnus Maurice Rose) the division reverted to U.S. Army Group command. Then it was no stopping the "Hell on Wheels" as it was the first U.S. division to reach the Elbe, and immediately put a bridgehead over the river in the confidence it could go on to Berlin. Of course it soon found that the Anglo-Americans were meant to stop at the Elbe and 2nd Armored's bridgehead, which had been deprived of air or other support, had to be withdrawn.

In sum, in a war as huge as the Allied struggle against Fascism in Europe, the public was relegated to absorbing the most skillful public relations experts who filtered events. And in the ETO the masters of publicity were Montgomery and Patton, temperamental

STATISTICS

Activated	15 Jul 1940
Arrived in North Africa	8 Nov 1942
Arrived ETO	24 Nov 1943
Arrived Continent (D+3)	9 Jun 1944
Entered Combat:	
First Elements	13 Jun 1944
Entire Division	2 Jul 1944

Casualties (approximate)	
Killed	1,162
Wounded	5,586
Missing	285
Captured	70
Battle Casualties	7,103
Non-Battle Casualties	7,116
Total Casualties	14,219

ASSIGNMENT AND ATTACHMENT TO HIGHER UNITS

DATE Assigned	CORPS Att'd	ARMY Assigned	ARMY GP Attached
24 Nov 1943		First	ETOUSA
27 Nov 1943	VII	First	
8 Feb 1944	XIX	First	
12 Jun 1944	V	First	
18 Jul 1944	VII	First	
2 Aug 1944	XIX	First	12th
7 Aug 1944	VII	First	12th
13 Aug 1944	XIX	First	12th
18 Aug 1944	V	First	12th
19 Aug 1944	XIX	First	12th
28 Aug 1944	XV	First	12th
29 Aug 1944	XIX	First	12th
22 Oct 1944	XIX	Ninth	12th
22 Dec 1944	VII	First	12th Br 21st
18 Jan 1945	VII	First	12th
16 Feb 1945	XIX	Ninth	12th Br 21st
4 Apr 1945	XIX	Ninth	12th
8 May 1945	-	Ninth	12th

opposites, each vying for supplies, priority and prestige. The 2nd Armored often found itself in a publicity vacuum, fighting under Bradley as opposed to the charismatic Patton; under the modest Hodges or newcomer Simpson; and most damagingly under Montgomery, whose operations most U.S. generals were anxious to disparage.

Though 2nd Armored fought titanic battles as a mainstay in the Allied line of battle throughout the ETO, it can be said that it only caught public attention when it broke free of Monty, the Rhine, and the envy of Third Army, when it raced to the Elbe, ahead of all other divisions under the skillful direction of Simpson's Ninth Army. It was only on this occasion, in fact, that Eisenhower finally acknowledged the 2nd Armored in his memoir. If Rommel, von Kluge or Model had survived to write memoirs, the 2nd Armored would have been featured more prominently.

During World War II, the 2nd Armored suffered 7,103 battle casualties (1,162 killed) and over 7,100 non-battle casualties, amounting to nearly a 100 percent loss of authorized personnel. Within the division, the 41st Armored Infantry had the highest rate of losses. It should be acknowledged here — as in every work on the war in northern Europe — that the infantry, especially the forward rifle companies, suffered the highest rate of attrition. 2nd Armored's most frequent partners in XIX Corps, the 29th and 30th Infantry, lost 204 and 185 percent of their establishments during the fighting, in battle and non-battle casualties.

At the end of the war the 2nd Armored Division not only broke through the German front but emerged from inter-army or inter-Allied infighting, and it was a measure of vindication that when the United States had a dire need to impress the Russians with a combat unit, "Hell on Wheels" was named the first American division to enter Berlin. After all its other "firsts," in North Africa, Sicily, Normandy, the Westwall, the Battle of the Bulge, the Ruhr Pocket and at the Elbe, this was a fine, though perhaps overdue, recognition for the 2nd Armored Division.

Below: Tanks race through Gross Gerau on their way to the industrial center of Frankfurt. The increasingly familiar surrender flags greet the troops as they pass through the town. *U.S. Army via Chris Ellis*

REFERENCE

INTERNET SITES

http://2ndarmoredhellonwheels.com
This is the official web-site of the 2nd Armored Divisional Association, with many categories of information and history and an interactive bulletin board.

http://www.gunts.net/army/2ndamr.html
Another site devoted to the 2nd Armored, with more of a post-World War II slant than the Association's. Contains fascinating stories about the Gulf War and prior.

http://www.globalsecurity.org/military/agency/army/2ad.html
Features a nice history of the 2nd Armored, and countless links to other units and personalities. The proprietors of this site should be commended for crispness and its attention to many facets of U.S. history.

http://my.oh.voyager.net/C8/07/lstevens/2nd/Index.html
Features a 36-page "Second Armored Division Booklet Published in 1945," compiled from contemporary U.S. news reporting on the 2nd Armored. The creator of the site, Larry Stevens, is to be highly commended for providing this rare look into the public perspective during the war.

http://www.army.mil/cmh-pg/
The excellent U.S. Army Center of Military History has a good section on 2nd Armored. Note also the full-text listing of Medal of Honor citations.

http://knox-www.armymil/museum/gspatton.htm
The Patton Museum of Cavalry and Armor is definitely worth a virtual visit if you can't get to 4554 Fayette Avenue, Fort Knox KY 40121. The museum's site identifies that it "displays German and Japanese war artifacts; an extensive collection of U.S. and foreign tanks and weaponry; and mementos of Patton's military career, including his wartime caravan truck and the sedan in which he was fatally injured in 1945. A battle re-enactment using World War II vehicles and equipment takes place on July 4."

http://www.reenactor.net/main_htmls/ww2.html
Reenactor.net provides links to a wide variety of WWII reenacting including 2nd Armored.

A View of Our Past . . .

General George S. Patton, Jr.
1885-1945

General George Smith Patton, Jr., was born on N[...] 11, 1885 in San Gabriel, California. His military c[...] one of the most colorful of all 20th Century milit[...] leaders. He participated in the Pentathlon of the [...] Stockholm Olympics in 1912 and placed fifth over[...] event. Later, he served as a member of General [...] Pershing's staff both during the punitive Expediti[...] Mexico and in World War I. He joined the newly [...] Tank Corps, where he served until the Corps wa[...] abolished in 1920 at Fort Meade, Maryland. Aft[...] War I, he held a variety of staff jobs in military [...] Washington, D.C., and completed his military [...] as the distinguished graduate of the Army Wa[...] He served as control officer for the mechanize[...] maneuvers in Georgia and Louisiana, which te[...] entire mechanized concept of the Army.

With the formation of the Armored Force in [...] Knox, he transferred to the 2d Armored Divi[...] Benning, Georgia, and was named the Com[...] General, 2d Armored Division, on April 11, [...] [...]vember 8, 1942, Patton commanded [...] in North Africa. After the [...] [...]forces in the [...]

Welcome to WWII Reenacting!

WWII reenacting has come a long way since its origins in 1975. Back then, it wasn't "cool" to cut your hair short or even to wear military uniforms. However, there were a group of guys who wanted to understand what it was actually like to really be in WWII. They rejected the "Hogan's Heroes" view of the war—instead, doing research, interviewing veteran's—it was a hard row to hoe and there were many pitfalls and false starts.

Finally, the "Morsels of Authenticity" page is going. Right now it consists of German articles, but we hope to have some other good ones soon. Especially on the Soviet Front. Also, the WWII Articles stuff has been separated into a new page, also appearing in the menu bar! The plan is, to update the After-Action Reports and things.

WE need your help to keep the lights on!
Our server bill has grown to a rather hefty size due to all the traffic we get [...]

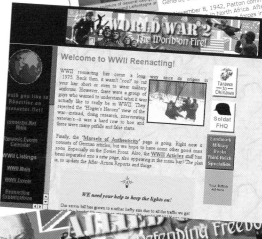

2nd Armor Division (USA CHG)--Located in California, this is the only armored unit in the CHG. They own a US halftrack and a few other toys.

4th Armored Historical Group (USA)--We are a group of WW2 enthusiasts who want to preserve the greatest time period of recent times. Through living history displays, we recreate what a camp setup would be lik[...]

SELECT BIBLIOGRAPHY

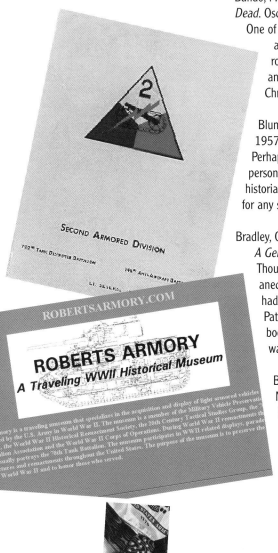

Bando, Mark. *Breakout at Normandy: The 2nd Armored Division in the Land of the Dead*. Osceola, WI: MBI Publishing, 1999.
> One of the best you-are-there WWII combat books ever written. Combines veterans' accounts with expert narrative and rare photos to illuminate 2nd Armored's role in Operation Cobra. A bonus, almost amounting to a detective story, is the analysis of the mysterious death/disappearance of Das Reich commander Christian Tyschen.

Blumenson, Martin. *The Patton Papers, 1940–45*. Boston: Houghton Mifflin, 1957.
> Perhaps the most valuable of all Patton books, because the snippets from his personal diary and correspondence are tied together by one of WWII's top historians. Blumenson's *The Duel for France, 1944* is also a sure-handed resource for any study of the ETO, from D-Day to the Westwall.

Bradley, Omar. *A Soldier's Story*. New York: Henry Holt, 1951; and (with Clay Blair) *A General's Life*. New York: Simon & Schuster, 1983.
> Though Bradley's war memoir is valuable and has slightly more campaign anecdotes, *A General's Life* is more honest. The latter was written after ULTRA had become public, and more importantly, after the memoirs of Montgomery, Patton, Eisenhower and others had been published. One thing that ties the two books together is the recurring theme that Bradley's greatest antagonist in the war wasn't Hitler, Rundstedt or Model — it was Monty!

Breuer, William B. *Operation Torch: The Allied Gamble to Invade North Africa*. New York: St. Martin's Press, 1985.
> Provides fine, often forgotten details about America's brief but sharp campaign against the French.

D'Este, Carlo. *Bitter Victory: The Battle for Sicily, 1943*. New York: E.P. Dutton, 1988.
> Admirably thorough, primarily from a command point of view, and frank about the campaign's middling outcome.

Dupuy, Trevor N. *Hitler's Last Gamble: The Battle of the Bulge, December 1944–January 1945*. New York: HarperCollins, 1994.
> Superb in both detail and analysis. The appendices alone are worth the price of admission.

Eisenhower, Dwight D. *Crusade in Europe*. Garden City, NY: Doubleday, 1948.
> Included here only for its curious uselessness. Between the spring of 1943 in North Africa and the withdrawal of its bridgehead on the Elbe in April 1945, the 2nd Armored is not mentioned at all, though Ike sometimes confuses it with the 2nd Infantry. In Normandy, Ike has the Culin hedgerow device shown to "Gen. Walter M. Robertson of the 2nd Division." The 2nd (and 3rd) Armored's role in the Battle of the Bulge is completely omitted. Kay Summersby could have written a better account of the war.

Elstob, Peter. *Hitler's Last Offensive*. New York: Macmillan, 1971.
An excellent work on the Bulge, especially noteworthy for a line of small print. After providing a rarely detailed account of 2AD's battle against the German spearhead between Celles and Dinant, including the role of five Shermans from the Royal Tank Regiment, a modest footnote says, "The author commanded one of those tanks."

Hastings, Max. *Overlord: D-Day and the Battle for Normandy*. New York: Simon & Schuster, 1984.
A masterful combination of intimate detail and strategic overview.

Houston, Donald E. *Hell on Wheels: The 2d Armored Division*. San Rafael, CA: Presidio Press, 1977.
The seminal published work on the 2nd Armored, written by a veteran of the division. Drawing on personal accounts, official reports and his own perspective, Houston provides a day-to-day look at 2AD from its formation to the end of WWII.

MacDonald, Charles B. *A Time for Trumpets: The Untold Story of the Battle of the Bulge*. New York: William Morrow, 1985.
Justifiably the most renowned book on the Battle of the Bulge, it nevertheless contains an error that symbolizes the way 2nd Armored's role in the battle has been neglected. Just when 2AD's massive Christmas attack to crush the German spearhead is being launched, a typo calls the division the "3rd Armored." Otherwise it's exemplary.

Below: On August 1, 1944, the day of the Avranches breakthrough, 67th Armored Regiment tankers reload their .30-cal. machine-gun belts. During the preceding few days, the division's CCB had played a primary role in springing Patton's Third Army from Normandy. *U.S. Army via Real War Photos*

INDEX